Courage to Train

Responsibility Delegated from God

Jeffrey A. Klick, Ph.D.

Unless otherwise noted, all Scripture quotations are from the ESV translation.

DEDICATION

To all parents that desire to make a difference in the next generation…And, to my daughter Sarah whose request is the reason for this book.

Table of Contents

ACKNOWLEDGMENTS

A very special thank you to my wife who remains my best friend after all these decades together…and to my wonderful children and grandchildren who were often the test subjects for much of this material.

Thanks, Joshua, for your continued assistance in reviewing and helping to find most of those many errors in my writing…

1. God's Way or Something Less

There is a way that seems right to a man, but its end is the way to death.
Proverbs 14:12

No one was paying attention as the three year old broke free from her father's grip and headed toward the busy road. Cars were racing by speeding to their destinations and the little child, getting close to the curb, was not easily seen between the parked cars. The father turned from the conversating he was involved in and saw his precious daughter getting ready to step into the street as he yelled her name…

What happens next?

There are no perfect parents only a perfect Savior. All the rest of us are in varying stages of growing up. Here is another truth - All parents train. We can't help it. The little ones that share our world are constantly observing our words, actions, attitudes and non-verbal communication. When we see an action or hear a word from the little mimics living in our home, we need to remember where they most likely heard or observed it first.

Children catch what is important to their parents, and they also discover quickly what we value. Our children will soon figure out when we mean what we say and when we don't.

Have you ever happened upon a disheveled mother counting loudly in the grocery store? As the toddler is disappearing around the corner, the mother is shouting out numbers to no one other than those watching her. I hope this is not you, but if it is, stay with me and I can help you get out of this embarrassing and frustrating situation.

I am not saying it is easy, but it is possible. Down through the centuries thousands of parents have accomplished this task – to train their children to listen to them and to respect their commands. You can do it too! There is a reason children are given to adults to raise and not the other way around, though both child and parent often do quite a bit of growing through the process.

The first questions we must answer are:

- What is our basis for truth?
- What is our standard of authority?
- Who or what are we going to listen to in order to train this new bundle of joy that has just arrived into our world?

Having often joked about the fact that children are born without an attached instruction booklet, I've come to realize that statement is not quite true. There are many voices available on child training, and we must choose between them carefully.

Two Schools of Thought

Each of us will decide which philosophy we will adopt. While there are many variations, I want to simplify them down to two options. First, we have human reasoning. From psychology to whatever current societal pressure is being pushed, this represents man's thinking at its best. It may be decorated with a scientific sounding name, or even clothed in pseudo love, but at its root it is human thinking. This is not necessarily all bad but limited in its scope, experience, and results.

This type of thinking would also include a reaction to whatever our own parents did or did not do as we were growing up. Perhaps they were overly strict or extremely lenient. Maybe they were abusive or negligent. We may adopt or avoid our parent's style of parenting and this is of course natural, but it is still based on human reasoning and personal experience.

The second choice is to follow God's Word and the clear instructions presented from the Creator of the human race. The One that created us male and female, boy and girl, and came up with the idea of parenting in the first place. For the record and just to make sure we are clear, this is the preferred model and the one I will be presenting in this book.

Yet there is hope, and it is in the Lord and His Holy Word.

It really does not take much effort to discover the results of following the first method. Simply turn on any TV, pick up any news magazine or tune into any daytime talk show, and the results will be painfully obvious. Our world is saturated with self-focused, self-centered, sinful creatures being raised by other self-absorbed humans.

The extreme edges of society have demanded normality in non-traditional marriage and gender identification, and have successfully argued that a sexual expression is now a civil right. Children are being purposely indoctrinated into anti-Christian thought from an early age. Parents are forced to deal with many destructive issues today as a direct result of our nation casting aside all Christian virtue and values. Yet there is hope, and it is in the Lord and His Holy Word.

Every parent will have to decide which of the two methods they are going to implement. As a Christian, I would argue for the God of the universe to know the right method. I would forcefully stress that

His timeless Word is still applicable today, and if we would return to the clear instructions within it, we would have much better results.

In the beginning of the human race, God created Adam and Eve. Genesis 2 and 3 are both very clear on the matter. I do not believe this is a fable, and I don't believe these are simply fantasy stories to make a larger point. I believe God actually created man and woman. I also believe God commanded them to be fruitful and to multiply, which means they were to produce children.

If we accept this premise, then it only makes sense that the One that created would provide instructions for the proper functioning of those creations. We have the Scriptures that most (I hope you are one of them!) Christians accept as the inspired Word of God. I am one of those types. I believe the Bible to be God's Word and to provide the instructions for how we are to live, and this includes marriage and parenting.

Most of us then would agree with these verses:

> For the word of God is living and active, sharper than any two-edged sword, piercing to the division of soul and of spirit, of joints and of marrow, and discerning the thoughts and intentions of the heart. Hebrews 4:12

> All Scripture is breathed out by God and profitable for teaching, for reproof, for correction, and for training in righteousness, that the man of God may be complete, equipped for every good work. 2 Timothy 3:16-17

Just from these verses it would seem those of us that believe in the truth of Scripture, should embrace the Word of God as the standard and practice for our lives and not settle for anything less. The Bible is meant to be our instruction book for all of life, and that includes the training of our children.

While many may argue over what the Scriptures mean and how they should be interpreted, most of the verses I will be sharing are not difficult to understand. The vast majority of the Word of God is clear and easy to grasp what it means This is especially true regarding marriage and parenting. The primary issues we struggle with are not the interpretation and clarity of the texts but implementation and obedience to them.

Take Ephesians 5:22-6:1 for example. These familiar texts are not difficult to understand. Words like love, respect, obey and such are well within our mental capacities to grasp.

The issue is not lack of understanding, but how in the world do I actually do it? How do I love my wife as Christ loved the church? How do I respect my husband when he frustrates me? How do children become trained to obey their parents in the Lord? These questions are not hard to understand at the root level, the difficulty comes in with implementation, not interpretation.

We first must make a choice in our marriages and in our child training as to which system we will adopt. We must decide whether God knows best or believe that some sort of a human system is better. We will implement a methodology and we will train our children. For the sake of the next generation, I pray we would choose wisely.

Our Choice Matters for Those that Follow Us

So, what happens to the little girl heading to the street when her father yells her name with a panicked voice? Depending on which system her parents had adopted to train her, she will either keep on running into the street and suffer the consequences, or she will stop immediately.

At these moments, life and death can hang on what we have chosen to do in our training. If you are familiar with toddlers and young children at all, you know they have high energy and can get in a great deal of trouble in a short amount of time.

When they are out of our sight, or it becomes strangely quiet, most parents know something is up! How we have trained our children to listen to our commands can have life-altering results.

Most children will find the pills or the cleaning supplies hidden under the counter at some point. Small children do not understand the dangers of knives, electrical outlets and cliffs. The water looks so pretty, and so does that animal with its large teeth. Children need parental restraint, and they need to be taught to listen when we give them commands. Their lives may depend on it.

Before we move along, I would ask you to stop and prayerfully consider some questions. Perhaps a time of discussion would be helpful in a small group or in your living room with your spouse and children.

Discussion Thoughts:

1. What did you like about your parent's training? What did you dislike? Why?

2. As you consider how you are training your children right now, which of the two methods mentioned are you following and why?

3. Do you like the results you are seeing so far? Why or why not?

4. Do you believe God's Word is true and is to be believed regarding child training? Why or why not?

~~~~~~

"Children are great imitators.
So give them something great to imitate."
Anonymous

"Children seldom misquote. In fact, they usually repeat word for word what you shouldn't have said."
Anonymous
~~~~~~

2. Authority

Let every person be subject to the governing authorities. For there is no authority except from God, and those that exist have been instituted by God. Romans 13:1

Someone is in charge of your home. There is a pecking order and there is a system in place of who decides what is decided. You may or may not be aware of it, but it is there. Decisions can and should be made on the basis of a plan, not out of frustration or manipulation.

The question I asked in chapter one applies here and throughout the rest of the chapters. What is your basis for truth? From your answer to that questions decisions and actions will follow. Who is in charge of your home? Who makes the decisions? Who determines bed times, what is eaten or not, what chores are accomplished or not? What is the atmosphere in your home? Cloudy? Stormy? Peaceful? Argumentative? Joyful? Christ-like?

No one likes to live under the thumb of a tyrant. A dominating, controlling, manipulating, always-angry ruler is no fun for anyone. While it is horrible if that describes one of the parents, it is equally awful if it is a child that is the ruler in the home. This seems to be the current human training choice - let the child rule!

Around the 1950's or so, some not-so-smart people claiming to be brilliant determined that it would be better for a child to rule the home than the parents. They did not directly come out and state such things, but the end result of their training proved their intent.

Parents that restrained any behavior in their children were told they would damage their child's psyche or limit their future creativity or ruin their self-worth. Even correcting the child could possibly do irreparable harm to the little darling and bordered on abuse.

The results achieved were what should have been expected when a society casts off restraint. Anarchy! Rebellion became the normal, default behavior, and we are still paying for this decision today. For centuries, parents restrained the unacceptable behavior of their children until the children were old enough to do so themselves. When the vacuum of authority was created by parents refusing to restrain, the children stepped in to fill the void.

A two-year-old tyrant is still a tyrant! A family being run by a toddler is out of order and follows the way of human thought, not the Biblical pattern for authority. God created parents first, then commanded them to be fruitful and multiply. God expects parents to purposefully train their own children in what is acceptable and unacceptable behaviors.

Children do not come out of the womb trained or restrained. Remember diapers? Most children are selfish, self-centered little humans that need a strong, loving hand of guidance, and God expects the parents to provide it until the child is able to do so themselves. The goal is to train early so the strong hand can be released as the child displays self-control and maturity.

While there are many Scriptures we could explore on this topic, I will provide just a few for your consideration:

> The rod and reproof give wisdom, but a child left to himself brings shame to his mother. Proverbs 29:15

> Whoever spares the rod hates his son, but he who loves him is diligent to discipline him. Proverbs 13:24

> Discipline your son, for there is hope; do not set your heart on putting him to death. Proverbs 19:18

> Folly is bound up in the heart of a child, but the rod of discipline drives it far from him. Proverbs 22:15

> Do not withhold discipline from a child; if you strike him with a rod, he will not die. Proverbs 23:13

> Discipline your son, and he will give you rest; he will give delight to your heart. Proverbs 29:17

> Fathers, do not provoke your children to anger, but bring them up in the discipline and instruction of the Lord. Ephesians 6:4

> Besides this, we have had earthly fathers who disciplined us and we respected them. Shall we not much more be subject to the Father of spirits and live? Hebrews 12:9

Even a quick reading over these verses will reveal that God expects parents to train their children and if we do there will be blessings – wisdom, love, hope, the removal of folly which will lead to "rest, and respect." If we fail to discipline them, then we are promised shame, hate, death, and lack of respect. Which do you want in your home?

So, back to the topic of authority and why it matters in child/parent training. Who is in charge in your home? Who should be? Does God really care and does He have any ideas for us to consider or obey? Again, the Scripture is clear.

> Let every person be subject to the governing authorities. For there is no authority except from God, and those that exist have been instituted by God. Therefore, whoever resists the authorities resists what God has appointed, and those who resist will incur judgment. For rulers are not a terror to good conduct, but to bad. Would you have no fear of the one who is in authority? Then do what is good, and you will receive his approval. Romans 13:1-3

Paul clearly states God is the One that established authority. Notice Paul's words – "every person," "no authority except from God," "whoever resists," etc. These are all far-reaching, all-inclusive concepts. It would seem this is not some general guideline to be ignored, but a principle to meditate upon and implement into our lives.

Some proudly place bumper stickers on their cars that shout "Question Authority," but Christians should be those that learn how to live and function under those in charge.

God has placed limits on authority and there are times when we must resist immoral or unscriptural commands from those in authority. We must obey God and not man, but in the vast majority of our conflicts, we are not being challenged to violate our faith, just our will.

There are five realms of authority: personal, family, church, governmental and employment, and are all places where authority functions. I believe we must begin to understand God is a God of authority and He delegates that authority to humans, including parents over their children.

God expects children to obey and honor their parents. In fact, He commanded it multiple places:

> Honor your father and your mother, that your days may be long in the land that the Lord your God is giving you. Exodus 20:12

> Honor your father and your mother, as the Lord your God commanded you, that your days may be long, and that it may go well with you in the land that the Lord your God is giving you. Deuteronomy 5:16

> For God commanded, 'Honor your father and your mother,' and, 'Whoever reviles father or mother must surely die.' Matthew 15:4

> Children, obey your parents in the Lord, for this is right. "Honor your father and mother" (this is the first commandment with a promise), "that it may go well with you and that you may live long in the land." Ephesians 6:1-3

> Children, obey your parents in everything, for this pleases the Lord. Colossians 3:20

God gave the fifth commandment in the Ten Commandments, repeated it in the second giving of the law in Deuteronomy, repeated it again through the teaching of Jesus and Paul and summed it up with "this pleases the Lord," in Colossians. It seems like God was serious about children learning how to honor and obey their parents.

Here is the issue though, the vast majority of children neither honor nor obey, nor do they wish to do so. Most children are self-focused and only want what makes them happy at the moment. Young children, and even self-trained older children, do not have the perspective or wisdom necessary to restrain themselves. It is clear God requires the parents to make up this lack of desire and assure the child(ren) learns to walk in God's ways.

God expects parents to help restrain the child's selfish behavior until they are old enough to willingly choose to do so. Children must be trained to honor and obey their parents, and God expects the parents to do the training.

If parents refuse to accept this command from God, then who will train the children? A lack of authority exercised by the parents will be filled by someone, so, who or what will do it? Peers? Books or the Internet? Facebook? The Military? The government schools? Other parents? Someone will fill the gap left by parents that refuse to take up the training mantle, but that is not what the Scriptures plainly teach. God expects parents to train their children.

If we take on the task of training our children there will be rewards and if we fail to do so, the opposite is also true – there will be shame. Training our children does not guarantee we will create perfect adults, but not training them will lead to many avoidable hardships.

Please prayerfully consider the passages I have already shared and consider the following points.

Discussion Thoughts:

1. What do you think about the word authority? Explain.

2. Why do you think God makes such a big deal out of submitting to authority?

3. Do you agree that God has delegated authority to parents to train their children? Why or why not?

4. How does a family function when a child is in control of it?

5. If parents do not train their children, then who do you think will?

~~~~~~

"Who can better tell what kind of dealing is fittest for children than God? Who can better nurture children than God?"
William Gouge (1575-1653)
~~~~~~

3. Accountability

His master said to him, 'Well done, good and faithful servant. You have been faithful over a little; I will set you over much. Enter into the joy of your master.'
Matthew 25:21

Someone has to be responsible. In our modern world accountability is almost a swear word. "It's not my fault, I'm a victim," shouts almost everyone when confronted about their behavior. Almost every parent that has more than one child has heard these replies. "He made me do it." "She started it." Sometimes the really brazen ones will even blame the parent. "It's your fault, I'm just like you!" "You were not clear enough." You get the idea. Very few people will willingly embrace personal responsibility.

Yet, God expects us to do so. While there are many applications to the parables Jesus told, one obvious fact runs through these:

- Matthew 24:45-51 – The Wise vs. Foolish Servant
- Matthew 25:14-30 – The Parable of the Talents
- Luke 16:1-13 – The Parable of the Dishonest Manager
- Luke 19:11-27 – The Parable of the Minas

God expects His people to be faithful with what they have been given, and there will be accountability for that expectation someday.

When we leave this life, I firmly believe we will spend some time reflecting upon and giving an account of what we have done with what we have been given. Our salvation is assured in Jesus Christ and His work upon the cross, but we continue to live a life of stewardship after we are born again.

Each of us has been given a gift of life and God expects us to do something with it. This is accountability. We will give an account of what we have done with this gift we received called life.

> For we must all appear before the judgment seat of Christ, so that each one may receive what is due for what he has done in the body, whether good or evil. 2 Corinthians 5:10

Parents are expected by God to train their children. We have been given a trust, a stewardship with these young lives, and God requires parents to do the job! We cannot delegate this task away, and we cannot blame anyone else if we fail. God holds parents responsible.

While that is a strong and somewhat scary sentence, we are not alone in the task. We have the Holy Spirit and the Word of God to lead, guide and empower us. God gave parents the task of investing in the next generation and we must take this task seriously.

We all know what it is like living in a culture where many parents have abandoned or have tried to ignore the assignment from God. Teenage crime and rebellion are at all-time highs. Disrespect for authority is rampant everywhere (including the home) and the results are damaging to all of society.

The reality that many children grow up in single-parent homes is a major problem, and even non-Christians know this to be true. God intended for parents to invest and train the next generation, and, currently, we are failing. Even in the Church. Even in godly homes. We must accept responsibility and we will face accountability for the decisions we make. God never required perfection, but He certainly does expect faithfulness.

> One who is faithful in a very little is also faithful in much, and one who is dishonest in a very little is also dishonest in much. Luke 16:10
>
> Moreover, it is required of stewards that they be found faithful. 1 Corinthians 4:2

God expects parents to train their children in His ways. Most of us are familiar with this passage, but I would ask you to read it again carefully looking for accountability in it:

> For I have chosen him, that he may command his children and his household after him to keep the way of the Lord by doing righteousness and justice, so that the Lord may bring to Abraham what he has promised him. Genesis 18:19

Do you see it? What if Abraham did not command his children and household? Would the Lord still have brought to him what He promised him? The "so that" in the verse seems to indicate a cause and effect situation to me. God expected Abraham to train his children and I would state that God expects each of us to do the same thing.

> Train up a child in the way he should go; even when he is old he will not depart from it. Proverbs 22:6

What does that verse mean if not responsibility? Who is supposed to train the child in the way he should go if not the parents? How will a child know what is right, proper, acceptable, and honorable if not learned through the parent's words and example?

Let me give you some verses for your consideration on this topic. I would encourage you to read them slowly and consider the concepts of faithfulness and accountability as you do.

> Only take care, and keep your soul diligently, lest you forget the things that your eyes have seen, and lest they depart from your heart all the days of your life. Make them known to your children and your children's children… Deuteronomy 4:9

> Hear, O Israel: The Lord our God, the Lord is one. You shall love the Lord your God with all your heart and with all your soul and with all your might. And these words that I command you today shall be on your heart. You shall teach them diligently to your children and shall talk of them when you sit in your house, and when you walk by the way, and when you lie down, and when you rise. Deuteronomy 6:4-7

> He established a testimony in Jacob and appointed a law in Israel, which he commanded our fathers to teach to their children, that the next generation might know them, the children yet unborn, and arise and tell them to their children, so that they should set their hope in God and not forget the works of God, but keep his commandments; Psalm 78:5-7

> Hear, my son, your father's instruction, and forsake not your mother's teaching, Proverbs 1:8

> My son, keep your father's commandment, and forsake not your mother's teaching. Proverbs 6:20

> Fathers, do not provoke your children to anger, but bring them up in the discipline and instruction of the Lord. Ephesians 6:4

Those passages should be sufficient to make my point. God told His people to make sure that their children understood Who He was and what He required.

God also instructed the children to receive and listen to their parent's instruction, and therein is often the battle. How do we as parents make our children listen? Part of the answer is in the passage from Ephesians 6:4 about not provoking our children to anger. I will explain how that happens in a bit, but for now, I will give you one word to consider – consistency.

Children need to observe parents being consistent. Our word should mean what it means and our temperament should be constant. Okay, don't shoot me, I am just stating we need to work on being consistent. We are all in varying stages of this process. Perfection is not required, but a direction is. We must learn to discipline, instruct, love and speak to our children in a consistent manner, so stay tuned for more insight on this topic as the book unfolds.

To summarize what we have learned so far:

- All parents train and God expects parents to actively participate in this process with their children.
- There are two basic ways to train our children – according to God's word or something far, far less.
- God has empowered parents with all of the authority they need to train their children.
- God expects parents to be faithful in their training, and we will give an account of how we did so when we leave this life.

While that list may seem daunting, by God's grace and with our faithful attempts to train our children, we will be successful. That doesn't mean we won't struggle or that our children will not cast aside our training when they are old enough to accept or reject it; it means

God expects us to do the best we can with what we know. In other words, He expects us to be faithful.

God expects us to do our best and leave the results in His capable hands. If we are faithful and attempt to be consistent, we will be so much further ahead than if we do nothing or pursue apathy in the training process.

There are no guarantees that our children will grow up and be perfect. In fact, I promise you they won't. However, we must do our best, pray for grace and invest in our children and their future.

We will give an account for what we have done and not for the results of what we have attempted. Each child will grow up and begin to make their own decisions, and they will give an account to God for these choices.

> God expects us to do our best and leave the results in His capable hands.

Perfection on the parent's part does not guarantee perfect children – remember Adam and Eve? God was the perfect Father, yet they chose to cast off their training and embrace sin. Our children can do the same. However, we must invest, pray, train and work with our children, for God not only expects us to do so, He commands it.

In all those stories I listed earlier about talents and faithfulness, the servants that received a rebuke were those that did nothing out of fear of the Master. The amount given was not the issue; it was what they did with it that merited either praise or condemnation.

The bottom line for parents is we need to exercise courage and faith when training and not cower in fear of failure or rejection. If we do our best under the leadership of the Holy Spirit according to God's Word, we will hear – "Well done good and faithful servant!"

Discussion Thoughts:

1. What does accountability mean to you regarding parenting?
2. How do being accountable to God and walking in grace mix together?
3. Why does God expect children to learn to listen to and obey their parents?
4. Are results and accountability tied together? Why or why not?

~~~~~~

"The greatest legacy one can pass on to one's children and grandchildren is not money or other material things accumulated in one's life, but rather a legacy of character and faith."
Billy Graham (1918-2018)

"It is easier to build strong children than to repair broken men."
Frederick Douglass (1818-1895)

"But for this purpose He has given us children, and issued this command that we should train and govern them according to His will, else He would have no need of father and mother."
Martin Luther (1483-1546)

"Begin early to teach, for children begin early to sin."
Charles Haddon Spurgeon (1834-1892)
~~~~~~

4. Training with Vision

If you know these things, you will be blessed if you do them. John 13:7

> Where there is no vision, the people are unrestrained, but happy is he who keeps the law. Proverbs 29:18 (NASB)

> Without guidance from God, law and order disappear, but God blesses everyone who obeys his Law. Proverbs 29:18 (CEV)

Other translations use thoughts like, "cast off restraint, run wild, abandon restraint, and shall perish," as a result of having no vision.

Vision may refer to prophetic revelation or God's Law, depending on the choice made by the translator. Both work great in my mind. The point is we need insight beyond our own understanding, and we should be directed by it!

In my corporate background there was a famous saying that went something like, "Aim at nothing and you will always hit it." We must have some sort of goal or purpose, or we are going to hinder arriving at any preferred destination with our training efforts.

Thinking about some goals, consider this list to begin:

- What do you want your adult children to act like?
- What set of values do you want them to adopt?
- What type of language do you want them to use?
- What about their attitudes?
- Do you want them to respect authority?
- Develop an excellent work ethic?
- How about their walk with God?
- The love for the Scriptures?
- Their view of the family?
- The Church?
- Life values?
- Usage of money?
- Future spouse?
- ___________ Fill in your favorite ones…

All of these and many more are important. How a child develops will largely depend on the influences and purposeful training they receive. We already looked at these verses, but take another glance at them:

> The rod and reproof give wisdom, but a child left to himself brings shame to his mother. Proverbs 29:15
>
> Train up a child in the way he should go; even when he is old he will not depart from it. Proverbs 22:6

Both of these passages lead somewhere. One leads to shame and one to acceptance of what was trained into a child. Which one do you want? How do you get there? If you don't know what you want, how will you ever know if you are making progress on the goal of achieving it? If you don't know where you are going in your training, you are left with random reactions and not any purposeful training. Perhaps even relying on anger or emotions instead of training.

If you want respectful children in word and deed, it will take training. If you want teenagers that are different than the ones that are self-trained, you must train them. Children left to themselves will not typically end up where you want them to be. Selfish children turn into selfish teenagers that turn into selfish spouses.

The self-focus that is natural must be trained out of a child, or it will have the potential to take over the adult they become. Of course, God can override poor training, and sometimes does, but, that does not mean we are relieved from the responsibility of training our children. We must train them or they will bring shame.

Selfish children turn into selfish teenagers that turn into selfish spouses.

If you don't believe children are selfish you probably have not had any yet. Simply tell an untrained child, "No," or, "Share," and see what happens. Or, place two children in the same room with one toy they both want and observe what takes place.

Have you ever met a young person that rolls their eyes every time they are asked to do anything they didn't want to do? How did they become that way? Why are there some young people that look you in the eyes and answer with a good attitude? Is it breeding or training? Did it happen by accident or did it take hours of training, discussing, and retraining?

I'm not talking about making robotic clones, but training with an end in mind when we begin. If we want well-adjusted, respectful young adults, we begin the process almost as soon as they are born. The longer we wait to adopt the Biblical method, the harder it becomes to correct inappropriate behavior.

A Brief Reminder

Before we delve into the deeper details, a reminder may be in order. There are no perfect children or parents. A child may be well trained and still choose to walk in sinful behavior, casting off all training when reaching an age of freedom. God the Father, Who is perfect, still had children who cast off His commands. While we, as sinful parents, will be grieved over some of our adult children's sinful choices, we are not responsible for their decisions. At some point they must take personal responsibility for going against how they have been trained.

In fact, if we reread Proverbs 22:6, we can see that there is a gap included there. A child may go through a time of testing, even rejecting what they have been taught, but they cannot ever escape from it. Even when they are old, the training is still there.

We are responsible to train and control what we can, but the child will grow into an adult and will be free to reject or repackage that training. If we have trained them, they can never get it out of their mind. No matter how old they may be. Don't you remember your parents talking to you, or at least remember their lives and the impact they made by their example? Your children will too when they are your age.

When you are considering having children, or perhaps when the cute little bundle of joy is in your arms, take some time and consider what you want this child to act like in 20 years. How will you help shape what is important in their life? What value system will they adopt? Will peers or family be more important? Will sports or the Gospel be first place? Money or service? How will they get to this place if you don't train them? While God's grace will redeem, it is Biblically obvious that God expects parents to be the primary shaping factor in a child's life.

Have you ever seen an out of control toddler, shouting, hitting, and screaming at their mother? How did they become like that? Who allowed them to display such behavior? The world would tell you that perhaps they have a mental disorder requiring medication, but is that even realistic? Yes, there are children that have extenuating physical or mental challenges, but is *every* child that displays a temper tantrum really mentally ill? Something is wrong with many of these children not afflicted with those challenges, and while medicine may dull the actions, it will not deal with the underlying cause.

The rebellious child does have an illness, and it is called sin and self-focus. Here is a thought to consider (again) – God expects you as the parent to restrain your child's words and actions until they can be taught to control them. If your child is out of control, how did they become so? What process took place for them to arrive at this destination? More importantly, can it be reversed or at least moderated?

Without a vision the people and children run unrestrained. With a vision there can be a well-trained, peaceful child sharing the home with their parents. There can, and should be respect, love, and teaching taking place with a vision being implemented.

Parents first have to decide what they want in their children's future, and then they have to adopt a Biblical plan to arrive at that destination. The majority of the time this will not happen by accident, but it can and will happen by working a plan of training. God's way leads to peace, but what many parents and children are experiencing is anything but peaceful.

God gives parents the right to establish rules and laws, and the power to enforce what is acceptable. Anarchy is not God's plan for the home. A home functioning in Biblical order will be substantially more peaceful than one saturated in rebellion and the overthrow of authority.

If you want godly teenagers, then begin today to train. If you want joyful toddlers, start now. If you want young adults that love the Lord, His Church, and ministry, they must be shown how and trained, trained, trained.

There are no guarantees in this world that all of our efforts will produce perfect results, but I can almost always promise you that if you do something it will work out better than doing nothing. If you have been doing everything wrong up to this point, continuing to do the same things will not help. Change must be made, and the sooner the better.

God is redemptive and He will take our efforts and multiply the results. We must begin somewhere, and I pray we would ask the Lord for the strength and wisdom to do so. A generation is waiting for parents to take their rightful place as role models, trainers and imparters of godly wisdom. May we accept the call!

Discussion Thoughts:

1. What do you think about the word vision?

2. Why is it important to have a vision regarding child training?

3. How would you like your children to turn out when they grow up? How do you plan to get there?

4. If there is still the chance that your child will choose poorly, then why should you bother with training?

~~~~~~

"The example of a father is acknowledged to be all-important. The stream must not be expected to rise higher than the fountain."
J. W. Alexander (1804-1859)

"I believe that Christian parents and children, Christian families, have a unique opportunity of witnessing to the world at this present time by just being different."
David Martyn Lloyd-Jones (1899-1981)
~~~~~~

5. Family Structure

When I was a child, I spoke like a child, I thought like a child, I reasoned like a child. When I became a man, I gave up childish ways. 1 Corinthians 13:11

Children do not come out of the womb already trained! A baby is different than a toddler who is different than a young adult who is different than an older young adult. That makes sense, right? Some parents seem to overlook this logical progression and understanding of growth in our children.

Treating a sixteen-year-old like they are five will breed rebellion and anger. Treating a five-year-old like they are sixteen is just as unwise. Every child matures at a different rate. If you are responsible for more than one, you already know this fact.

Myriads of studies attempt to explain the reason for this reality by references a variety of causes, from birth order to inherited personality traits, to societal or economic conditions. I'm sure each of the studies have some measure of truth. For our purposes, let's just agree that there is no one-size-fits all approach, and every child is a unique creation made in God's image.

Every child will most likely challenge their parents. There are very few passive, always-obedient children. Most have a will and probably a strong one. Humans always do, and our children are human. Do not be surprised when you observe anger, selfishness, disrespect, rudeness, or any other undesirable behavior in your child. When Adam chose to sin, death was unleashed, and it continues down to our current day - no one is immune.

Because there are no perfect children, God decided that parents should train and restrain the child until they are old enough to choose to do so themselves. Most children will not choose to do so willingly but will need to be instructed and disciplined into doing so.

Not to be overly redundant, but if you desire to confirm what I just wrote, stop by just about any store and simply observe an out of control toddler screaming, crying, demanding and controlling their harried parent. An untrained child will become self-trained, and it rarely ever is for the better. Parents are to be the restraint until the child can restrain themselves.

Remember chapter one about choosing God's way or something less? Hang on, because here we go into waters that will surely make some angry and others scream child abuse! We must decide how we will train our children, for all parents' train. We must decide whose instructions we will accept and whose we will reject.

For hundreds and thousands of years, parents used corporal force in the training process. In the 1950's, Dr. Spock (not of Star Trek fame, but the humanist psychologist), among others, came out strongly against this practice claiming restraining the child would cause serious damage to the child's psyche. The child's self-esteem would be damaged, and the child would become a serial abuser.

Time has shown that rejecting God's Word and adopting a humanistic replacement has produced several self-absorbed generations that have a poor work ethic, little value for human life, no respect for the elderly, a self-focused value system, disregard for marriage, and distain for most traditions.

The parents that adopted the anti-Biblical view produced the Boomers and hippies, who produced the Generation X (latch key) group, who produced the Millennials, who are producing the Generation Z folks who are almost completely absorbed in cell phones and technology.

Neither spanking nor corporal punishment is child abuse.

There are sufficient jokes and YouTube videos already available that show the flaws of each of these generations, so I won't reproduce them here. Some are funny, yet most are sad if we stop to think about them.

My main point is we have taken a great step backwards from previous generations that learned how to work, became self-sufficient, that were willing to die for their country, stayed married, and valued something beyond their own pleasure and satisfaction.

My wife and I were watching a mini-series on the life of John Adams, and I remember his conversation with his fourteen-year old son. The father said something like, "Son, you're fourteen, and it is high time for you to begin to give back to your country in service what you have received." John Adams was sending his son to become an ambassador to France. Times have changed, and I would argue not for the better! So, what has changed?

At least part of the answer is that parents have chosen to reject God's Word and adopt a humanism-based replacement. If this is even remotely true, and I firmly believe it is, then the logical step is to reverse this choice made by previous generations by returning to God's Word as our instruction manual for child training.

One issue to really start up an intense conversation is spanking. In our day, is it even possible to use corporal punishment without ending up in prison for child abuse? While we need to be wise and aware of our surroundings, the answer is yes. And I believe we must if we hope to stop the journey away from truth into error.

Neither spanking nor corporal punishment is child abuse. Of course, it can be if taken to extreme measures, but simply obeying the Scriptural commands is not abuse. A spanking given in love while not angry is a training method and is not abuse. Any parent that would abuse their child is not walking in the Holy Spirit but in sin and needs to repent. If they refuse to repent, then the full power of the law should be brought down upon them. Saying that, however, does not mean spanking is abuse. I would argue that not disciplining a child is far closer to actual abuse.

Please consider God's Word about the topic before you react to what I have written so far:

> The rod and reproof give wisdom, but a child left to himself brings shame to his mother. Proverbs 29:15

> Whoever spares the rod hates his son, but he who loves him is diligent to discipline him. Proverbs 13:24

> Folly is bound up in the heart of a child, but the rod of discipline drives it far from him. Proverbs 22:15

> Do not withhold discipline from a child; if you strike him with a rod, he will not die. If you strike him with the rod, you will save his soul from Sheol. Proverbs 23:13-14

> Even though I walk through the valley of the shadow of death, I will fear no evil, for you are with me; your rod and your staff, they comfort me. Psalm 23:4

> And have you forgotten the exhortation that addresses you as sons? "My son, do not regard lightly the discipline of the Lord, nor be weary when reproved by him. For the Lord disciplines

> the one he loves, and chastises every son whom he receives." It is for discipline that you have to endure. God is treating you as sons. For what son is there whom his father does not discipline? If you are left without discipline, in which all have participated, then you are illegitimate children and not sons. Besides this, we have had earthly fathers who disciplined us and we respected them. Shall we not much more be subject to the Father of spirits and live? For they disciplined us for a short time as it seemed best to them, but he disciplines us for our good, that we may share his holiness. For the moment all discipline seems painful rather than pleasant, but later it yields the peaceful fruit of righteousness to those who have been trained by it. Hebrews 12:5-11

How can we read all those passages and not arrive at the conclusion that God wants us to discipline our children, using a rod when necessary to achieve that purpose? The Lord loves us and disciplines us; should we do less for our own children?

Child:

Biblically speaking there seems to be only two stages – children and adults. "Teenager" and "adolescence" are terms not found the Bible. There are children and there are adults. By creating an artificial third group we allow children to remain in that stage for an extended period of time and sometimes, they do not grow out of it at all.

A recent national headline about a thirty-year-old man sued by his parents to evict him from the house is all the buzz in the media. How sad on multiple levels. It's a tragedy that his parents didn't train him to accept personal responsibility at a young age.

Babies are just that, babies. Attempting to spank a baby is simply not appropriate. That does not mean that a baby can or should be given everything they demand through crying and fits. Babies need holding, food, warmth and love.

Babies also scream and demand nearly constant focus. Some of this is normal, but a discerning parent will recognize very early when a baby has a need or is simply expressing anger. While not an exact science, having been around my own three babies, and now thirteen grandbabies, I can testify that all babies want what they want when they want it, and most will not naturally patiently wait.

They can be trained to wait and they should be. If you give in to a fit when they are a baby, the temptation is to give up training and allow the child to set the tone in the house. This is a mistake. Soon after the baby arrives, schedules can and should be set in motion, and what is acceptable and unacceptable should begin to be explained. All babies cry, but they don't have to be allowed to scream in anger. Your behavior and response will quickly train the baby as to what is acceptable and what works. They are typically quick learners!

> It is at this stage that a child will learn what your word means. Or not.

Babies quickly become more mobile and turn into crawlers, climbers, and toddlers. I believe if parents would invest the most time in training in this stage, the best long-term results would be achieved. It is at this stage a child will learn what your word means. Or not. Does "no" mean "no," or simply a "yes" if I scream, cry, pout, or ignore the word? You will train your child what your commands mean by how you ignore or enforce them. Choose wisely.

Children will quickly learn what you really mean when you say, "don't touch," or "don't move while I change your diaper," or "come here," or "stay in bed," or "take at least one bite," etc. What does your word really mean to the child? How will they know? How can you assure them that you mean what you say when you say it?

Does counting work? Maybe, but when we count what we are really saying to our child is that our word does not mean what we say until we reach some number. Does a time out work? Perhaps, but a little break in the corner or in a room is not too bad of a price to pay in order to get my way instead of listening to yours! How do we enforce our will when there is a clash of wills? Corporal punishment.

The only really fair way to train a child is to teach them that your word means what you say the first time you say it. If you have to raise your voice, threaten, count, or distract, you have already lost the battle of wills, and it is always an issue of wills. Whose will is going to be enforced in the home?

I hope by now that the many verses I have provided will convince you God expects your will to be enforced and not that of a self-centered, self-gratifying, disobedient child. We all tend to gravitate to selfishness and God disciplines us. He expects us to do the same for our children.

When there is an issue of wills, your will must be enforced. The child must choose to obey or endure the appropriate level of discipline when they willingly choose to ignore or disobey your will. If your will is rejected and there are no consequences we have what is commonly called anarchy. An overthrow of government has occurred, and you, as the parent, encouraged and allowed it.

Most children will respond to a stern command, a light swat, or, as they age, a strong spanking. The sooner you start the quicker the pattern can be established. What will you allow? What is your tolerance level for obedience? Is rebellion something that you desire? The only fair way for the child is to establish the guidelines and then to enforce them consistently.

While no parent is completely consistent, we need to strive to be so. Our word should mean the same thing each time we issue a command. If it does not, then the child becomes confused and the boundaries blur. Children need to understand what the boundaries are and what are the consequences of breaking them. Start young and the process gets easier as the child learns you mean what you have stated.

Spanking, grounding, and even withholding money are all acceptable methods of discipline for a child. As a child ages and shows maturity, the rules and methods must change. For example, spanking an older child is insulting, and giving commands without explanation or reason works great when a child is three or four, but to a young adult it is completely out of line. The young adult needs to understand the "why" behind the command, and this will take time and discussion.

Age Differences in Families

Some families are large and some are small. Some will have adult children living under the same roof as newborns. Other families will have siblings that are not related living in a blended family. Each of these situations provide challenges and opportunities for the training and discipling of the next generation.

As with everything else we have discussed so far, one size does not fit all. If you have a twenty-something young adult still in the home and you just had a newborn or are dealing with small toddlers, this can be stretching!

How do I give the time necessary to the young adult and yet oversee and work with an active child? How do I resist the temptation to delegate the training to the older children? It is not wrong to train older children to assist the parents, but replacement should not be an option. God expects parents to train their own children, not the older sibling.

This mixture within a home provides excellent growth opportunities for all involved! Both parents and children can be stretched and develop life long bonds of friendship.

Time is, of course, a fixed commodity, but it seems to be in short supply! If you find yourself in a situation where there is not enough time to accomplish all that needs to be completed, then steps must be taken to prioritize what is really important.

Having taught time management courses in the past, almost everyone faces challenges in dealing with too much work versus too little time to do it. The only solution is to evaluate what is really important and plan your schedule accordingly.

This is where reviewing the chapter on vision might be helpful. If our vision is set regarding what we want to accomplish, then it becomes a bit easier to reduce the distractions that are time-stealers. We are always going to be tempted to give time to the tasks that are less important, and we must learn how to win this battle.

What really is important in your life? Is having a personal devotion time with the Lord and the Word of God? Is investing in the lives of the children? Is spending time with your spouse? Is discipleship? We all will make time for what we value.

That is not to say that there won't be periods of our life when we are stretched, for there will be! But, even in those harried times we will make daily choices as to what we want to do. In short, we will find time to do what we want to do.

Young adults need time to talk and discuss what is going on in their lives and small children need nearly constant oversight. How do we do both? Excellent question!

Perhaps some planning would help in answering this issue. Maybe a date night could be scheduled for a time of discussion between the parents. Written communication could be used to help focus discussions and helps us think deeper. Sometimes sleep just needs to be put off for what is important. We will spend our time and money on what we value, and investing in our children is far more important than entertainment and even free time. Yes, we need a break sometimes, but discipling our children is really important.

Our older children and younger ones need our time, focus, and attention. Communication is helpful and can be used as a training tool during these times. The young adult can learn patience and how important child training is and can also set an example to follow for the younger children.

The young child can also learn patience and that the entire world does not revolve around them and their needs and can glean wisdom from the more adult conversations.

If death to self and love for others are both taught and practiced, great growth can and will occur. Lifelong relationships can be established and wisdom can be imparted across the age gaps. Young children naturally look up to the older ones and the positive impact made can be substantial.

For parents of children of multiple ages, of course, there will be times of stretching and being overwhelmed, but the interaction and time together can also be a tremendous blessing!

Families can laugh, worship together, discuss deep topics and learn to enjoy the relationship growth. Yes, there are dangers of giving the adult children too little time or too much authority over the younger children, but life is often messy. If we have messed up somewhere along the lines, then we need to change our behavior and not be overly discouraged about it. We are not perfect and never will be. God expects faithfulness not perfection. We all will fail but we are not failures in Christ! We are His beloved children.

The mistakes we made in training our older children don't have to be repeated in the younger ones. We can listen to comments from the older ones and, instead of defending and reacting, hear the truth and change. Comments like, "you never let us get away with that," or, "why do you not deal with that disrespect?" can be challenging and also insightful, if we don't react.

God is the One that put your family together, and He has wonderful plans for it! He should be the center of the home and the underlying purpose for everything that takes place. What a great goal!

Whatever the makeup of your family, time has shown that everyone will grow up, and the current situation is not the last one. Our challenge is one of learning how to enjoy the time we have now and not lose it to regret over the past or fear of the future.

Most friends come and go but our family will be family forever. Therefore, we must learn to enjoy this gift from God!

Blended Families:

This term often refers to second marriages and children living under the same roof that have different parents. Sometimes through death or divorce, new families are created. This can be both a blessing and also a challenge.

The blending of families brings challenges due to different backgrounds and training. Mixing young adults that are not related presents sexual attraction and temptation issues. The parents will, of course, refer to the young adults as brother and sisters, but they are not blood relatives, and hormones often rage during these years. Ignorance and refusal to consider sinful behavior has led to many heart breaks. Open communication and safe guards must be set in place to assist in the normal battle of sexual attraction.

The blessings can include an expansion of ideas, values, and training possibilities. The truth is we are all adopted into our Father's family and we are all a blended family in some degree! We can and must learn to love those who are different from us, and a new family will provide multiple opportunities to do so.

Children will need to be trained to respect the parent that is not theirs but is now in a position of authority through the new marriage. This can be challenging and we all know the stories of step-mothers and how wicked they can be…Why is it always step-mothers anyway?

Regardless of your answer to that question, issues will arrive with not being the biological parent. "You are not my real mother or father," is often yelled by a hurt, angry teenager. The response to this reality by both parents is important. A unified message is critical for success.

Time does help to heal wounds, but so do comforting words, humility, and listening to a hurting person. Much discussion and effort will be required to help smooth the transition to this new normal in the family unit.

The non-biological spouse will need a sensitive heart, a listening ear, and strong support from the other parent. A divided house will not stand, so unity is imperative in these type situations. Children learn quickly which parent can be manipulated and which one resists. Both parents need to be unified and supportive of one another. All rebellion, hateful comments, and attempts at division need to be dealt with quickly and lovingly.

Before moving on, let's stop a minute and consider the following:

Discussion Thoughts:

1. What do you think the Bible means by the usage of the term "rod?"

2. Why are children selfish, sometimes cruel, and often out of control?

3. Why do you think the world system is so opposed to corporal punishment?

4. How is being consistent a key in child training and necessary to bring peace to a home?

~~~~~~

"Learn to say "No" to your children. Show them that you are able to refuse whatever you think is not fit for them. Show them that you are ready to punish disobedience, and that when you speak of punishment, you are not only ready to threaten, but also to perform."

J. C. Ryle (1816-1900)
~~~~~~

6. A Battle of Wills

Finally, all of you, have unity of mind, sympathy, brotherly love, a tender heart, and a humble mind. 1 Peter 3:8

If you are observing your children, the inevitable will happen. Your child will display behavior that is not acceptable. By starting the training process when your child is very young, you will save yourself great amounts of work later in your efforts to control their sinful nature.

As revealed in chapter five by the Scriptures shared, I believe spanking is a normal, Biblical form of discipline. I also believe that spanking should be reserved for rebellion. In addition, there are other forms of correction and discipline for lesser infractions that we will discuss later.

Rebellion takes place when children communicate in some fashion, "No, I will not do what you want." Now, they may say it outright, or they may say it with an attitude, or they may simply choose to disregard what you have said; but make no mistake, that is what they are saying.

When there is an issue of wills, the parents must win every time. Have I said that before? Do not let your child's will be established as the final authority in these cases, but insist your will be carried out completely without backtalk. Remember, children must be trained to carry out your wishes, and this will go against their natural desires. Granted, there are some children who are more passive and agreeable, but all children have a will that must be brought under the authority of the parents. When the inevitable conflict arises, what should be done? I am glad you asked!

The first step in training is to make sure the child understands what is expected. Most children understand much more than their parents give them credit. Toddlers understand a great deal of what you are saying. "Go get your blanket," and the child retrieves it with little difficulty. "Don't touch" or "no" is something else the child should learn very early.

I have seen pre-walking children told, "Do not touch the book," and they look at their parents, then at the book in question, then back at their parents, and then touch it to see what will happen to them. If nothing happens, a small victory has been won for the child, but a major defeat has been suffered by the parent. The parent is training the child that their word means nothing. If, on the other hand, discipline follows the act of disobedience, the child learns there are consequences to his behavior. A child learns quickly whether his parent's word can or should be trusted.

A Conflict Example

Make sure your children understand what you expect by clearly telling them. If they are old enough to talk, have them repeat it back to you. If they are not yet talking, have them look you in the eyes and make sure they understand what you are saying. Remember, unless there is some mental incapacity, the child learns quickly what you want and knows a lot more than you think.

Once the child understands and then chooses to disobey your will, the battle of wills begins. In the example above, the child (we will call him Bobby) understood he was not supposed to touch the book but decided to test the parents. After the child touches the book, the parents should firmly say, "Bobby, I told you no. You need to obey Mommy (or Daddy)," and remove the child's hand from the book.

Some children will respond to the verbal correction, and that is fine. Most will not. The child will again touch the book and look at the parents to see what happens next. Repeat, "I told you no and that you must obey me." What takes place next is very important, and will go a long way toward establishing the spirit of your home. Another rebuke will probably not change this persistent child's behavior. Stronger methods are usually required.

I strongly recommend acquiring a "rod" very early in the child training process. Why a rod? Because that is what the Bible clearly commands, and that should be a good enough reason for Christians. We often get into failing situations when we think we know better or more than the Scripture. Reread the verses in the previous chapter. The word rod is used often and is there by God's design.

> If you lose the battles when they are two, you will lose the war when they are fourteen.

Children need to know what the rod is for and how it will be used. The rod should be with you always when you are training. A child will quickly understand that the rod will be administered whenever disobedience arises. Rods can be a dowel rod, a switch, even a wooden spoon if it is sturdy enough, but something that will inflict enough pain without causing damage to the child's physical body. The point of using the rod is to change the child's behavior, not inflict pain. Pain is simply the tool used to persuade children that the parents' will is better than their own will.

Since the child refused to leave the book alone after the rebuke, then a spanking is in order. The issue is not the book but the will. Some parents at this point think it is easier to move the book and simply avoid the conflict. While this may be true when a child is a toddler, they are setting a disastrous training process in motion.

This avoidance of the conflict will tell the child your word does not mean anything, and if he persists, he can usually get his own way. While this may seem petty when the child is a toddler, the real fruit of this will manifest itself when the child is older. If you win each battle when the child is young, you will have far fewer struggles when the child is older. The opposite is true as well; if you lose the battles when they are two, you will lose the war when they are fourteen. A properly trained toddler will grow into a delightful teenager, and a wild, selfish, uncontrolled toddler will grow into…

Another topic that arises here is the subject of grace. Wouldn't it be more Christlike to simply give the child a break and let it slide? After all, God does not always instantly deal with all of our issues.

Grace is given by God, but He is perfect, understands fully the consequences of His actions, and knows completely what He is doing. We do not. I am all for grace, and each situation must be evaluated, and giving your child a break now and again during the training process certainly is acceptable.

Conversely, giving grace in almost every situation because we are tired or don't want to deal with the underlying issue will not produce the type of fruit we desire. God does give us grace; however, He never winks at sin. The price paid for our sin was high, and it should never be taken as a license to have our own way. Disciplining our children is a God-given command, and we cannot ignore it under the guise of grace. There are times when it is better to hug and laugh, but these should not replace the training process.

Discipline involving spanking should be an event not a reaction. A spanking should be given in private without anyone else watching. This is a time of training, loving, and cleansing and is a very private matter. This is not a time of screaming, fighting, struggling, or providing a spectator sport for other children.

Take the child to a private place, sit him down, and explain exactly what he did wrong. Young "pre-speaking" children need simply to understand that obedience is the standard and they did not obey Mommy or Daddy. If they are old enough to talk, do not ask for an excuse, for you will always get one. Do not ask, "Why did you touch the book?" or "Why did you do that?" Ask, "Do you know what you did?" or "What did you do that you were told not to do?"

Explain that you love your child and God requires that you make them obey. Make sure they look you in the eye and do not allow them to struggle with you. Warn them they will get extra swats for struggling, kicking, screaming, etc., and then follow through if they do not listen. It will usually only take a time or two, and they will calm down and actually receive the spanking without a fight.

A child knows when they have done something wrong; therefore, the guilt that follows must be dealt with in an appropriate manner. Spanking provides the necessary cleansing that must take place to restore the relationship between the child and parent. This principle is demonstrated in Scripture by the following:

> But your iniquities have made a separation between you and your God, and your sins have hidden his face from you so that he does not hear. Isaiah 59:2

When we sin, our relationship with our heavenly Father is hindered. We are not kicked out of the family of God, but our intimacy is damaged until we deal with the sin. A separation happens between God and us because of our willful disobedience. Jesus took our shame and guilt by His death on the cross, and therefore forgiveness is available. Our responsibility is that we must confess our sins and receive forgiveness and restoration so that we can restore the lost intimacy with our Father. The same principle applies with our children's sins against us. They must be confessed and dealt with in order to regain the normal relationship.

The confession of the disobedience and the subsequent discipline remove the guilt and restore the relationship. When we fail to follow this pattern, we make room for distance in our relationship between our children and ourselves. Resentment often follows, and a further breakdown of the relationship is inevitable.

On the other hand, following through with consistent discipline actually promotes closeness and love. One of our adult children came to us and said, "When we were young every time you spanked us, you said you did it because you loved us. I didn't believe you then, but now I know you did. Thank you for spanking us!" Most parents would love to have such a conversation; we certainly did! My child's understanding of the discipline is based on the Biblical principles that were commonly understood for thousands of years.

Recently, many have accepted the counterfeit belief system presented by the culture around us that spanking and discipline are actually harmful to the child. Consider this verse from the book of Hebrews:

> For the Lord disciplines the one he loves, and chastises every son whom he receives. It is for discipline that you have to endure. God is treating you as sons. For what son is there whom his father does not discipline. If you are left without discipline, in which all have participated, then you are illegitimate children and not sons. Hebrews 12:6-8

Chastise is not a common word in our day, but the definition can still be found. Most dictionaries will define the word as "To punish, as by beating. To criticize severely; rebuke." I am not advocating beating children; however, I am saying the Bible instructs us to discipline our sons and daughters and to use whatever force is necessary to win the battle of the wills. The above verses clearly state love and chastisement go hand in hand. In addition, if discipline was not given, it was understood the child was not even a real son or daughter, for every father disciplines the children he loves.

Fearing our children will not love us when they grow up if we restrain and spank them is unfounded and unbiblical. Children actually feel unloved if the parents do not even care enough to tell them, "no," or to stop them from inappropriate behavior. Parents who fear losing their children because of disciplining them, most often *do lose them* to others that will challenge them. Many unrestrained young people rebel by running off to join the Marines or even extremely controlling cult groups that will offer them discipline. The child knows he needs boundaries and will seek them from others if parents do not provide them.

Some in our day shout that spanking children is the equivalent of beating, abusing and performing violence against our children. The logic follows along the path that by "hitting" our children we are training them to become abusers and we are, in fact, abusing our children.

I am not suggesting that we beat our children, nor am I promoting abuse in any fashion. As the following example will show, corporal punishment is not violent, nor abusive, but actually loving. Many abusers and violent adults today grew up in homes where there was no discipline or restraint at all, thus invalidating the argument against spanking. The rates of murder, violent crimes, and the like have increased under this line of thinking, not decreased, as the non-Biblical methods of discipline have become the norm. Before accepting the world's mindset, we must examine their thinking through the grid of Scripture and reject what is unbiblical.

An Example of How to Administer a Spanking

After an event when the child has clearly chosen to break your understood command, remove the child to a secluded place. Breathe deeply to gain self-control and try to remember the goal of what is about to happen.

You are not randomly inflicting pain on the child, but you are attempting to set a pattern of obedience to authority that will last the rest of the child's life. Have the child look you in the eyes and explain to them what happened and why you are going to spank them. Depending on the age of the child, either have him lie across your lap or bend over a bed or chair.

Next, using a rod, firmly strike the child on the buttocks, not the legs, back, face, or any other part of the body. The number of swats should be in direct proportion to the level of disobedience. The issue is breaking the will and gaining submission, not inflicting pain and suffering on the child.

A child who can speak will most likely beg for the spanking not to take place and plead that he is really sorry for the offense. The sorrow is wonderful and necessary; however, the fulfilling of the discipline is just as important. We must teach our children there are consequences for the decisions they make.

The point of a spanking is deterrence, and the pain must be sufficient to make the child choose the parents' will over their own the next time he is faced with this choice.

Parents who complain that spanking does not work are usually not administrating it properly or consistently. Again, assuming there are no inherent mental limitations, success will follow, for a spanking is supposed to hurt more than the child's choice, thus providing incentive for the event not to be repeated.

If a child laughs or an acts like the spanking does not hurt, it is not being performed properly. Many parents swat a child on a diaper, and while it may sound loud, it has little effect on the child. When a child is small, the spanking should be given on the bare bottom. As the child ages, on the undergarments is sufficient. After the event, lots of hugs and kisses should be given to assure the reestablishment of the relationship. Make sure the child understands you love them and this ends the event. As you can tell, spankings take time and should be an event to make an impression that lasts beyond the conflict. If spankings are given when needed and consistently administered, the frequency will decline as the child ages.

We had strong-willed children (really it seems all children are strong-willed!), and we spanked them often. One of our children needed a spanking for refusing to play nicely with a child we were babysitting. This child of ours refused to share and was displaying a very nasty disposition.

We instructed this child as to what we expected, and she refused to listen. Therefore, a spanking followed. After a discussion of what was expected, the child was marched back into the room and given the opportunity to apologize. This child folded their arms and refused. Shocked, I marched this one back into the room and gave another spanking. The scene was repeated with the opportunity to apologize given again with the same result. This little two-foot-tall rebel crossed their arms and flatly said "no."

All the time and effort we invested in training our children is paying dividends in the next generation.

It took several spankings to break this rebellious attitude. Finally, after what seemed like hours, this child broke and gave in. I firmly believe that if we had let this child win this battle, we would have suffered significant damage in the war of wills. This was one of the defining points in this child's character development and ours. This was the only time a repeated battle was required. There were more battles but none like this one. I wonder what would have happened had we allowed this child to win. As I walk around grocery stores and see two-foot-tall rebels screaming at their mothers, I really do not have to wonder much. Such rebels are trained to be self-absorbed by the failure of their parents to restrain them.

These training experiences take time, energy, and patience, but they are well worth the reward of having peaceful, obedient children. As I observe my adult children train their own children using the same techniques, my heart is warmed. All the time and effort we invested in training our children is paying dividends in the next generation.

Children are very smart and they will test the parent's resolve—sometimes just to make sure they really mean what they have said. When you begin to train your children, do not be surprised if they test you in front of people or out in public. The child wants to know how much they are really loved, and your response in these situations will communicate greatly to your children. Are you really willing to walk out of a restaurant and go home or to the car and deal with a child throwing a temper tantrum? Will you leave a cart full of groceries at the checkout to restrain a rebel? Will you deal with the bad attitude when the grandparents are over? How about when your friends are over and you are busy talking and the child wonders, "Will you stop and deal with me?" Children will test your resolve and commitment to disciplining them.

If we are inconsistent or lazy, the child will know it and be insecure.

If we will deal with each instance of rebellion, the child will be secure and feel protected and will stop testing you as often. It is a perfect match, for children inherently want to be disciplined and told what to do, and God wants the parents to do it.

One question that always arises is "How old should a child be when we begin to spank, and when should we stop spanking?" I mentioned before that a discerning parent can detect when a baby is angry and when there is a legitimate need. I am not recommending that you spank babies; however, even a baby can be trained to lie still for a diaper change by simply swatting their bottom when they attempt to roll away. Certainly, by the time children are mobile, they are ready to be trained, and hopefully the process is in full action before they are toddlers.

The upper age depends on the maturity level of the child involved. Modesty issues need to be considered, and the humiliation process must be evaluated when spanking an older child. There is no absolute answer as to an upper age when it comes to spanking, but if the parents are consistent and have captured the battle of the wills while a child is young, there may not be much need for spankings after the first few years of a child's life. On the other hand, some children need firm discipline for years and years. The simple answer is, it all depends.

Is it all worth it? If you are consistent in your love and discipline, your children might just thank you when they are older. Even if they don't, God expects us to train and discipline our children. Parents who die to themselves and invest the time necessary to train their children are setting themselves up to reap a reward of a lifetime relationship with their adult children. From personal experience, I can tell you it is well worth whatever time and energy expended to have an excellent relationship with your children and grandchildren!

Discussion Thoughts:

1. Why is every discipline battle an issue of wills?
2. Why is it so important for the parent to win every battle?
3. How do grace and discipline intersect?
4. How is discipline of our children an act of love?

~~~~~~

"If you are driven to the rod, then strike advisedly in a calm frame of mind, and soberly show them their fault,; how much it is against your heart to deal with them int his way; that what you do, you do in conscience to God and love to their souls; and tell them that if they had done the right thing, none of this severity should have been."
John Bunyan (1628-1688)

"Children should be trained up in the way of self-denial. As without something of this temper, we can never follow Christ or expect to be owned by Him as His disciples, so neither indeed can we pass comfortably through the world."
Philip Doddridge (!702-1751)

"If you would have your children obedient servants of Christ, you must govern them well. Submission to authority is one grand law of His Kingdom. Implicit obedience to your authority will well accord with the submission your child must render to Christ."
Edward W. Hooker (1794-1875)
~~~~~~

7. God's Promises if We Accept

If you love me, you will keep my commandments. John 14:15

God's Word is clear on most topics. People fuss and fight about some of the minor points, but most of us understand enough to be successful.

If we obey what we understand and actually attempt to put it into practice, Jesus states that we are wise builders that have chosen to construct something that will withstand the storms of life.

> Everyone then who hears these words of mine and does them will be like a wise man who built his house on the rock. And the rain fell, and the floods came, and the winds blew and beat on that house, but it did not fall, because it had been founded on the rock. Matthew 7:24-25

We also know that those that choose to disobey the clearly revealed will of God are not wise. I'll cover this sad truth in the next chapter.

God Expects Us to Obey Him:

> Now therefore, if you will indeed obey my voice and keep my covenant, you shall be my treasured possession among all peoples, for all the earth is mine; Exodus 19:5

> Be careful to obey all these words that I command you, that it may go well with you and with your children after you forever, when you do what is good and right in the sight of the Lord your God. Deuteronomy 12:28

> And Samuel said, "Has the Lord as great delight in burnt offerings and sacrifices, as in obeying the voice of the Lord? Behold, to obey is better than sacrifice, and to listen than the fat of rams. 1 Samuel 15:22

> So you shall keep my commandments and do them: I am the Lord. Leviticus 22:31

> Whoever has my commandments and keeps them, he it is who loves me. And he who loves me will be loved by my Father, and I will love him and manifest myself to him. John 14:21

> If you keep my commandments, you will abide in my love, just as I have kept my Father's commandments and abide in his love. John 15:10

There are of course many more verses that are clear, and the goal of these few is easy to understand – obey the Lord! We know these things, but living it out in our daily lives is often a challenge.

Even from these few verses it is clear if we walk in obedience God promises many things including:

- We will be His treasured possession
- It will go well with us and our children
- We will be loved and see God more clearly
- We will abide in God's love

From the opening pages of our Bibles, it is clear God expects His people to walk in obedience to His commands even if we can't see or understand all the reasons why. There are great rewards for walking in faithful obedience. This is also true for parents that wonder if what they are doing is really worth it.

Consider the following verses specially through the lens of being a parent.

> The proverbs of Solomon. A wise son makes a glad father, but a foolish son is a sorrow to his mother. Proverbs 10:1

> A wise son makes a glad father, but a foolish man despises his mother. Proverbs 15:20

> Let your father and mother be glad; let her who bore you rejoice. Proverbs 23:25

> Discipline your son, and he will give you rest; he will give delight to your heart. Proverbs 29:17

The wisest man of the Old Testament, Solomon, wrote these words. If we raise wise children then we will have hearts full of gladness. Gladness means a deep happiness and contentment. Is all the effort worth it? Do we want to be full of gladness and enjoy our days? Of course!

The last verse above ties together discipline and rest leading to delight! When we follow God's ways we will receive what God has promised. A disciplined child will be one at rest which leads to the parents also entering into delight over their child or children.

> Behold, children are a heritage from the Lord, the fruit of the womb a reward. Like arrows in the hand of a warrior are the children of one's youth. Blessed is the man who fills his quiver with them! He shall not be put to shame when he speaks with his enemies in the gate. Psalm 127:3-5

Who does not want a heritage? While not a word we use all that often, it speaks to leaving something behind us that has value. Most people desire to be remembered for something worthwhile. The Scriptures here state that children are something of value given to us by our Lord.

Blessed often means happy and one that receives favor. Our children are called that! The Psalmist also states we are blessed if we have these arrows. The number is not important, the fact of the gift is.

Our enemies will not bring us shame because of this heritage from the Lord. If we do well in raising our children, and by "well" I mean following the Master's Handbook, our enemies will not triumph over us. That is a blessing indeed!

We can also consider some of God's promises to parents regarding our efforts and the fruit that awaits our obedience:

> Train up a child in the way he should go; even when he is old he will not depart from it. Proverbs 22:6
>
> Rejoice in the Lord always; again I will say, rejoice. Let your reasonableness be known to everyone. The Lord is at hand; do not be anxious about anything, but in everything by prayer and supplication with thanksgiving let your requests be made known to God. And the peace of God, which surpasses all understanding, will guard your hearts and your minds in Christ Jesus. Philippians 4:4-7
>
> All your children shall be taught by the Lord, and great shall be the peace of your children. In righteousness you shall be established; you shall be far from oppression, for you shall not fear; and from terror, for it shall not come near you.
> Isaiah 54:13-14
>
> Your wife will be like a fruitful vine within your house; your children will be like olive shoots around your table. Behold, thus shall the man be blessed who fears the Lord.
> Psalm 128:3-4
>
> Then he brought them out and said, "Sirs, what must I do to be saved?" And they said, "Believe in the Lord Jesus, and you will be saved, you and your household." Acts 16:30-31

God has promised many things to His faithful servants. As parents we are given a gift of stewardship over these precious children. We are not alone, however, for the Lord is with us! His grace is always sufficient and His Word is true.

We can train with confidence that God will use even our mistakes to His glory, for nothing is wasted in His Kingdom. We can rejoice in the Lord and receive peace even in child training for God has promised it.

We can share the Word of God around the table with our children, and we can discipline them in love. God will complete His work, for so He has promised. While we certainly are imperfect, He is not. The Scriptures are clear regarding our charge to teach and train:

> Fathers, do not provoke your children to anger, but bring them up in the discipline and instruction of the Lord. Ephesians 6:4
>
> And these words that I command you today shall be on your heart. You shall teach them diligently to your children, and shall talk of them when you sit in your house, and when you walk by the way, and when you lie down, and when you rise. Deuteronomy 6:6-7
>
> Whatever you do, work heartily, as for the Lord and not for men, knowing that from the Lord you will receive the inheritance as your reward. You are serving the Lord Christ. Colossians 3:23-24

Parenting takes faith, courage and humility. We need faith to believe God's Word is true and the correct way. We need courage to continue on even though everyone else is walking in some other direction. We need humility to embrace obedience even when we can't see or understand everything.

God has promised to never leave us or forsake us and everything will work out for good sooner or later and these promises must include parenting! (Romans 8:28)

Here is one more insight into parenting, (which includes spiritual children as well). This elderly apostle towards the end of his life shares the fountain of his greatest joy:

> I have no greater joy than to hear that my children are walking in the truth. 3 John 1:4

Probably in his nineties, John the apostle of love, states there is no greater joy than hearing that his children are walking in Jesus' way. What a summary of a life! What will bring us the most joy as we face leaving this earthly life? Not money, success, houses, land or anything temporal, but knowing that those who follow us are walking in the truth! This is a great reward for faithfully living, sharing and investing in those that come after us.

Discussion Thoughts:

1. Why does God expect us to obey Him?
2. How can raising children lead to joy, love and gladness?
3. How are children a heritage from the Lord?
4. Is God reliable regarding His promises to us? Why?

~~~~~~

"If you neglect to instruct [your children] in the way of holiness, will the devil neglect to instruct them in the way of wickedness? No; if you will not teach them to pray, he will to curse, swear, and lie; if ground be uncultivated, weeds will spring."
John Flavel (1628-1691)

"1. Subdue self-will in a child and thus work together with God to save his soul. 2. Teach him to pray as soon as he can speak. 3. Give him nothing he cries for and only what is good for him if he asks for it politely. 4. To prevent lying, punish no fault which is freely confessed, but never allow a rebellious, sinful act to go unnoticed. 5. Commend and reward good behavior. 6. Strictly observe all promises you have made to your child."
Susanna Wesley (1669-1742)

"Let no Christian parents fall into the delusion that Sunday school is intended to ease them of their personal duties. The first and most natural condition of things is for Christian parents to train up their own children in the nurture and admonition of the lord."
Charles Haddon Spurgeon (1834-1892)
~~~~~~

8. God's Promises if We Refuse

Be not like a horse or a mule, without understanding, which must be curbed with bit and bridle, or it will not stay near you. Psalm 32:9

We briefly looked at the positive promises for investing in training our children in the last chapter. Now let's get a bit negative. We can learn from both good and bad examples. I pray we choose to imitate the excellent ones and reject the foolish ones.

We all make a choice regarding what we will do. This is true in our behavioral choices and how we will go about exercising parental stewardship. While God has entrusted us with the responsibility to train our children, He does not force us to walk in wisdom in doing so.

Will we choose to follow the Scriptures or will we not? The Bible from cover to cover is a long, sad tale of the people of God walking away from their loving Father.

Beginning in Genesis with the first couple's failure to obey and ending in the final judgment revealed in Revelation, humans have continually refused to accept God's commands as the proper way to actually live their daily lives.

The Children of Israel struggled with taking on their neighbors' false religions, and we do the same in our day. While we are not serving Baal or some ancient false deity, how often do we take the word of someone saturated in secular humanism as truth on how to train our children? How often do we allow the government schools, TV shows and the internet to train our children?

Sometimes we abdicate our responsibility and then wonder why we achieve the results of that choice. Questions are asked like, "Where did we go wrong?" and statements made like, "If I had to do it all over again I would…" Wouldn't it be better to attempt to follow the guidelines established by God Almighty in the first place?

Of course there is hope for those of us that have failed. God is redemptive, and His grace is lavished upon us! God can and will redeem, and that story runs right alongside the tragedy of choice made by all of those in the Bible.

From Genesis to Revelation God has been offering redemption to His people. Jesus' mission was to seek and save the lost, and God so loved us He sent His Son to die for us to make the way of salvation to anyone that calls upon Him. Grace, mercy and love flow from the heart of God!

We all have failed and fall short, so don't read the following verses as hopeless but as a warning to make a right choice. When we fall, and we all do, we run into the arms of Mercy and find hope and help in our time of need.

With that being said, however, the right and best choice is to avoid the sin and mistakes in the first place by choosing to heed the wisdom from the Scriptures.

> The proverbs of Solomon. A wise son makes a glad father, but a foolish son is a sorrow to his mother. Proverbs 10:1
>
> A foolish son is a grief to his father and bitterness to her who bore him. Proverbs 17:25
>
> He who does violence to his father and chases away his mother is a son who brings shame and reproach.
> Proverbs 19:26
>
> The rod and reproof give wisdom, but a child left to himself brings shame to his mother. Proverbs 29:15

What a sad list these four verses include – sorrow, bitterness, shame, reproach, and more shame. All of these outcomes are a direct result of how the children act.

If our children end up fools, (not mentally, but spiritually), how did they arrive there? If they are allowed to bring violence to their parents, who gave them permission to do so? If they are left to themselves, being deprived of the rod's wisdom, who made that choice in the first place? There are some self-trained children that end up making the right choices, but the Scriptures are clear regarding the normal outcome of parents not training, and it is not a pleasant thought!

Not every child that is disciplined ends up walking with God, and the opposite is also true. However, that does not mean we as parents have the right to disobey God's clear commands to train our children. We do what we are told to do, and then we are not responsible for the results of our children choosing to reject the training we attempted to give.

God will lovingly deal with our sons and daughters that go against their training, for He loves them far more than we can. Our job is to do the best we can accepting the stewardship we have been given.

Our children may rebel against their training, but they will know the way they should go and we have seen that God's Word states they will not get away from it!

Just because the possibility of our children rejecting our training as they leave our homes exists, this does not alleviate our responsibility to perform it. God has given us a charge, and He expects us to be faithful in fulfilling it to the best of our abilities.

I don't want to spend a great deal of time on the negative results of our failure to train, but let me end this chapter with the opposite side of John's source of great joy.

> I have no greater joy than to hear that my children are walking in the truth. 3 John 1:4

If John received no greater joy by his children (both natural and spiritual) walking in the truth, then the other side of that is true as well. There is no greater pain, sorrow and heartache than to see our children walk in lies and errors.

As our children leave our home and start out on their journey of life, it is often a fearful thing for concerned parents. How do we know they will choose well and wisely? What will happen to them if we are not there to protect and warn them?

Faith must be front and center in a parent's life. We must believe that God is more than able to take care of our children as they leave the protection of our homes.

None of us will ever have done enough to prepare our children for life. All of us will have failed at some things and, most likely, at many tasks. Our children will have to learn to make it the same way you and I do – through faith and trust in our God and relying on His grace, mercy and forgiveness.

There are not spiritual grandchildren where God is concerned. He is the Father, not the grandfather. Each son and daughter must have a personal relationship with God through Jesus empowered by the Holy Spirit - just like you and I must have one.

We know this truth in our minds, but sometimes our hearts overwhelm us with fear, worry, doubt and dread. The answer for these issues resides in the same place as all others we've discussed – in God's Word.

Prayerfully consider these passages when fear and doubt overwhelm you concerning your children or your parenting skills. While there are hundreds you could focus on, this sampling can and will bring peace to your heart and mind if you believe.

> …for God gave us a spirit not of fear but of power and love and self-control. 2 Timothy 1:7

> For you did not receive the spirit of slavery to fall back into fear, but you have received the Spirit of adoption as sons, by whom we cry, "Abba! Father!" Romans 8:15

> I have said these things to you, that in me you may have peace. In the world you will have tribulation. But take heart; I have overcome the world. John 16:33

> There is no fear in love, but perfect love casts out fear. For fear has to do with punishment, and whoever fears has not been perfected in love. 1 John 4:18

> You keep him in perfect peace whose mind is stayed on you, because he trusts in you. Isaiah 26:3

> And which of you by being anxious can add a single hour to his span of life? Matthew 6:27

> And we know that for those who love God all things work together for good, for those who are called according to his purpose. Romans 8:28

The bottom line of this chapter is both a warning and an attempt to encourage. We are responsible for training our children and there are consequences for not doing so.

Our children can bring joy or shame to us by how they live. When they are in our homes under our direct influence, we should be able to instruct and train them in the correct way to live.

As they mature and gain freedom and eventually move out to begin to establish their own homes, our direct responsibility and influence changes. We become counselors (if they wish for it) and we release them into and under God's parenting.

Discussion Thoughts:

1. Why does God want us to obey Him?

2. How can raising children lead to shame, sorrow, and emotional heartache?

3. If children can grow up and reject our training, why bother in the first place?

4. How do you deal with fear, worry and doubts?

~~~~~~

"The primary lesson for life must be implanted in the soul from the earliest age. The primary lesson for children is to know the eternal God, the One who gives everlasting life."
Clement of Alexandria (150-215)

"With us everything should be secondary compared to our concern with children, and their upbringing in the instruction and teaching of the Lord." John Chrysostom (347-407)
~~~~~~

9. Personalities

For just as the body is one and has many members, and all the members of the body, though many, are one body, so it is with Christ. 1 Corinthians 12:12

I've often said that if two people were exactly alike one of them is not necessary. Like any master craftsman or artist each work created by them is unique. God is the Master Creator and each one of us is a masterpiece. We are by design very different from one another, but why would we expect anything else?

We have twin grandsons and observing them for a minute or two will prove my point. Though they may look alike, they are vastly different in humor, temperament, and personality.

If you have more than one child you already know this to be true. Behavior we tend to get used to when our firstborn comes along, gets totally blown out the water with the second. The third and following children will also be vastly different.

If we attempt to use a one-pattern-fits-all type approach in discipline and training, all involved will end up frustrated. No two children are exactly alike, therefore, no single method will work with every child.

There are of course some things that need to stay the same.

- We must be consistent with our commands.
- We should be clear and make sure our commands are understood by the child.
- Rebellion must be dealt with quickly.
- We must not show favoritism.
- We shouldn't compare a child to their sibling. Ever. Never.

Each child is a unique gift from God and made in His image, therefore they have worth and purpose. Each one should receive our love, time and attempts to understand them as a unique masterpiece in process.

In addition to the above few points, we must understand that each child will hear and see things differently. Don't husbands and wives? Why wouldn't children? What is obvious to one may not even be noticed by another. Many times there are issues that are not right and wrong but right and left!

Some children are creative and some logical. Some emotional and some with little discernable feeling. Some are relational and some are not. Some extroverts and others prefer to be alone. Which one is right and which one is wrong?

We had three children we raised and now are enjoying thirteen grandchildren with number fourteen on the way! Each one is different and a unique expression of God's creative ability. Some love animals, some are allergic to them. Some faint at the sight of blood, others love to watch stiches being sewn. Several love math and others prefer to write. Most like to be outdoors, but some prefer a good book in a comfy chair. Again, which ones are right and which ones are wrong?

Gaining an understanding of our child's personality at an early age will help us with the training process. Are they strong willed or more compliant? Are they outwardly honest but inwardly a liar? Do they sweetly rebel or are they defiant? Every child sins and all of them need training.

The job of the earnest parent is to train them up in the way they should go according to Proverbs 22:6. Some have explained the word "train" can refer to an ancient technique of "touching the pallet" with some sort of food.

While it may seem a bit gross in our day, in ancient times a mother (or whoever was charged with taking care of the small child) would chew some of their favorite food and then place it on the tongue of the child. Ignoring the amount of germs being transmitted for a minute, the goal was to help the child develop a taste for what the parent liked.

We can relate to this in thinking about what we expose our children to in order to help them gain a taste and desire for it. We need to choose wisely regarding exposing our children to events, activities and entertainments for which we don't really want them to develop a taste for it. Repeated exposure will help create a desire.

The latter portion of the often used passage in Proverbs 22:6 refers to the "way they should go." "Way" here is often explained as "bent," or "how they are made." As wise parents we will invest time and energy into finding out what motivates our children. What inspires them and what does not? What way should they go when they mature and reach adulthood? What are they really good at and what do they struggle to accomplish?

For example, if your child is very creative, perhaps their "way they should go" is more in the arts arena – drama, music, writing, etc. If they love logic, math or science, then perhaps something more technical is in order.

Some children love to build and others love to take things apart. Both can find their way in more hands-on type outlets. By way of reminder, which one of these choices is correct and which one is wrong?

As parents, part of our early job is restraining rebellion and helping to provide self-control for our children. The bulk of our training comes after we accomplish these. We must spend the time to get to know what makes our child unique. One size does not fit all.

Disciplining Differing Personalities:

Some children can break down and cry when a parent simply raises their voice or gives them a stern look. Others are going to need much more hands-on discipline, pun intended.

The Scriptures provide some warnings especially to fathers:

> Fathers, do not provoke your children to anger, but bring them up in the discipline and instruction of the Lord. Ephesians 6:4
>
> Fathers, do not provoke your children, lest they become discouraged. Colossians 3:21

It is interesting that both of these commands are directed to fathers. It is clear from these two verses that the father's behavior and attitude can have a dramatic impact on the lives of his children.

We can provoke them to anger and we can lead them to being discouraged. Neither of which is what we would ever want! We must learn how to deal with each child and learn what works and does not – an inexact science at best! Often we discover what is good through trial and error, therefore humility and forgiveness must be given freely on both the father's and child's part.

As we enter the discipline stage each child's personality must be evaluated. To the stubborn, leader type, we can tend to be more direct and firm. To the tender follower type we need to be more comforting and assuring. We must pray for wisdom and guidance from the Holy Spirit to reveal to us how best to navigate these waters.

Rebellion needs to be addressed quickly regardless of personality. Defiance of authority, whether clothed in smiles or feigned emotional responses, has to be put down completely. The differences resided in *how* we deal with, not *whether* we do or not. We must deal with all rebellion, and the sooner the better for all involved.

After we discipline, some will need longer comfort times than others. All will need love and assurance that their behavior failure does not exclude them from being part of the family. Everyone needs love and assurance, even the strong, but especially the weak.

Sometimes it seems parents spend all day breaking up fights between siblings. A good understanding of personality differences will help in this arena as well.

As parents we should refrain from comparing our children to ourselves or to a sibling. Each child is a unique gift from God and should be viewed as such.

Naturally, we will see our own faults in each child and we will also notice the differences between children. The value and worth of each child is what I am referring to here. Different is not bad, it means it is just not the same as the other, and that is by God's design.

Perhaps God in His sovereign knowledge knew exactly what He was doing when He gave you the child or children that He did. What an understatement! But sometimes we tend to forget Who is the Author of life and the One that gave us these blessings called children.

Since most of us would believe that God is Sovereign, it would stand to reason that He gave us just the right offspring to bring about His eternal will and purpose. Our job as parents is to discover how to help our children know the Father and lead them to the Throne of Jesus. Discipleship, service, love, grace, mercy, forgiveness, and all manner of spiritual growth begins at home!

God has built into the family unit the processes of discipleship and spiritual growth, just by nature of our daily living together. Learning to walk in love, which is our calling card to a lost and dying world, begins in the home (John 13:34-35).

Differing Personalities Are Excellent Marriage Preparation:

Since each person is unique and because these individuals dwell under the same roof, the opportunity for growth and training is immense. We often told our children they would most likely grow up and marry someone with the personality of one of their siblings. This proved to be the case.

God provided multiple learning opportunities within our home for each child to learn how to work through relationship conflicts with their sibling in preparation for marriage.

It seems to be the case that many people will marry someone with a different personality to the one they have. Introverts are drawn to the extrovert and messy people tend to end up marrying organized ones.

Many times these types of differences are seen in the people growing up together, and these differences provide a wonderful chance for growth and developing relationship skills. Learning how to get along with a sibling is often God's way to help a child prepare for a lifetime of marriage.

A wise parent will notice the differences and help explain them to the children. Just because someone sees things in a different way does not mean they are wrong. We all need to grow and none of us is the sum total of all wisdom and right thinking.

Helping our children learn to give grace and even grow to where they can enjoy the differences instead of always fighting about them, will go a long way to helping them get ready for a life partner. No matter who our children end up marrying, they will have a different personality. We can and should help our children prepare for this truth. (See the appendix for further discussion regarding future spouses.)

Find Out What Type Personality Your Child Has:

Discovering what your child's personality is early on will help with fulfilling the "way he should go" part of Proverbs 22:6. Each child is a gift and a masterpiece in process given to the parents and family from God Almighty.

God is not a sadist nor does He give bad gifts to us. If you are struggling with a child's personality (or your spouse's for that matter) then perhaps a change of perspective is in order.

Each of us tends to believe we are correct in all matters. Our view is the right one, and if everyone would simply see things our way all would be well.

While few of us would ever say such things out loud for fear of being called arrogant and full of pride, how could it be any other way? Which one of us willingly clings to a wrong opinion? Who among us, on purpose, makes mistakes and believes lies? We all think we are right, or we would change our minds to the correct view.

Herein lies the problem. All of us can't be right, and none of us has all of the proper views. God, in His infinite wisdom, knows this and therefore provides people to us to help us grow. This most often shows up in their holding different opinions or personalities.

From a young age, we are faced with a decision – do I fight and fuss with everyone who is different than me, or do I learn to embrace and grow to appreciate those differences? Guess which answer is the right one!

We, as wise parents, must learn to appreciate those differences in our spouse and in each of the children God gives us. Then, we must begin to teach our children what we have learned to help prepare them for life.

They will all encounter others that are different in personality and many times will end up marrying one of them. Learning how to deal with this issue at home will help prepare them when they establish their own households.

There are many free tests available online if you want to pursue learning about the different personality traits. The corporate world spends millions of dollars each year in attempts to figure this out so they can get the most out of the workday. Shouldn't we spend some time to understand this concept at home?

Here are some popular tests that you can take that will give some insights into why each member responds (or not) to various situations. There are free versions via the web that are fun and will prompt many discussions!

- DiSC Personality Profiles
- Myers-Briggs
- Five Big Personality Traits
- 16 Personality Factor Questionnaire
- Love Languages – Gary Chapman

While these tests will give some insights, they are simply tools.

God expects His children to grow and change as we all learn how to mature in love one towards another.

My appeal in this chapter is for parents to learn to appreciate the differences and help the children do the same. We must be sensitive to the differences between the children and help them see the differences as a gift from God, not something to be competitive over or to covet.

God did not make a mistake in putting together the various personality differences within your home. In fact, He gave everyone a gift! His desire is that all involved would learn to grow in love and patience, and differences are just what the Creator ordered!

Discussion Thoughts:

1. Why do you think God didn't make us all alike?

2. How can discovering the different personality traits in our family help grow and develop love?

3. What is the danger of comparing one child to another?

4. How could learning to get along with a sibling help in a future marriage?

~~~~~~

"You cannot but own that it is a matter of vast importance, that your children be fitted for death, and saved from hell; and that all possible care be taken that it be done speedily; for you know not how soon your children may die. Are you as careful about the welfare of their souls as you are of their bodies? Do you labour as much that they may have eternal life, as you do to provide estates for them to live on in this world?" Jonathan Edwards (1703-1758)

"There is much of God's providence exercised in and about children." Thomas Manton (1620-1677)
~~~~~~

10. Rebellion vs. Childishness

Brothers, do not be children in your thinking. Be infants in evil, but in your thinking be mature. 1 Corinthians 14:20

By now it should be obvious that if we are going to do a good job in training our children, we are going to spend a great deal of time on the effort.

In addition, it should be apparent we are going to make mistakes. There is only One perfect Man and we are not Him. One mistake to avoid is treating every childish act as rebellion.

I firmly believe spanking should be reserved for overt rebellion and not for every infraction of our endless rules. I also believe in authority and the establishment of boundaries. Obedience should be expected and enforced, but joy and laughter ought to be the normal atmosphere of our home. Peace, joy, rest, and a relaxed mood should be what our home is known for and not a tense hotbed of anger and legalism.

By attempting to defeat rebellion when our children are very young we can and should pave the way for a free-flowing, loving relationship between family members. No one likes to live in a home where one has to walk around in fear and wondering when the other shoe is going to be dropping.

It may seem illogical to state that if we are strict disciplinarians early we will be much more relaxed as the child matures, but that is exactly what I am saying.

If we are diligent when our children are young, we are preparing for a much easier and far more delightful relationship as our children move into adulthood.

The goal is to let up on our heavy-handed training as soon as possible, not to control the actions of our maturing children. We are their self-control *until* they are able to control themselves, and the sooner they are successful the better!

We put down rebellion in every case when our children are young. As they mature, we give them more and more freedom with an eye to releasing them into the world as ambassadors for the Kingdom as soon as they are ready.

One issue we may confuse is the difference between a child being rebellious and simply being a child. A child may drop their food on the floor because they are being rebellious, or they may simply be curious.

A spilled glass of milk is a mess to clean up, but how often is it knocked over due to rebellion against your authority? Perhaps they simply knocked it over because they were not paying attention. Should you spank a child for being childish or for being too young to know they would hit the glass with their elbow if not careful? No.

We must cry out for discernment in child training. Many unnecessary wounds can be given by assuming the worst about our children and their motives.

Yes, children can and do rebel. This clear attempt to overthrow authority must be put down. But, children are also children and are often just showing how young and immature they are and this type of behavior does not need a spanking. It still needs to be addressed, but spanking is reserved for rebellion and should not be the default recourse for every infraction of the rules.

Of course children need to be trained to be more careful. They need to understand that when they throw a ball towards a window or at a decoration it can break. There are consequences to actions like these, but these are not typically rebellious behaviors; they are simply childish.

Training to Reach Wisdom:

Remember a few chapters back when I said we should have a vison for our training? One excellent goal or vision to pursue is to have wise children. When our children leave our homes will they be wise or will they be something far less than that?

It's not a stretch to say many young adults are far from wise. Many employers bemoan the lack of quality workers that will take initiative and give a full day's work for the equivalent pay.

Studies have shown many college graduates of our day could not pass an eighth grade test of generations past. Education has been dumbed down, and so have expectations for young adults.

Some of the trend is tied back to the false understanding of the teenage years in which we do not challenge our young people to step up to adulthood. In addition, many parents in our day seem to want to relive their lives through their children so they simply don't challenge them to grow up.

When it comes to training the next generation we need to expect more from our children, for they are starting out further ahead of where many of us began our journey to adulthood. We all pray our children will far surpass us in wisdom, success, and impact with their lives.

The Bible is clear as to where wisdom comes from and to its advantages. Consider this sampling of passages:

> So teach us to number our days that we may get a heart of wisdom. Psalm 90:12

> The fear of the Lord is the beginning of wisdom; all those who practice it have a good understanding. His praise endures forever! Psalm 111:10

> For the Lord gives wisdom; from his mouth come knowledge and understanding; Proverbs 2:6

> Blessed is the one who finds wisdom, and the one who gets understanding, Proverbs 3:13

> The beginning of wisdom is this: Get wisdom, and whatever you get, get insight. Proverbs 4:7

> Say to wisdom, "You are my sister," and call insight your intimate friend, Proverbs 7:4

> The fear of the Lord is the beginning of wisdom, and the knowledge of the Holy One is insight. Proverbs 9:10

> Wisdom rests in the heart of a man of understanding, but it makes itself known even in the midst of fools. Proverbs 14:33
>
> Listen to advice and accept instruction, that you may gain wisdom in the future. Proverbs 19:20
>
> Yet among the mature we do impart wisdom, although it is not a wisdom of this age or of the rulers of this age, who are doomed to pass away. But we impart a secret and hidden wisdom of God, which God decreed before the ages for our glory. 1 Corinthians 2:6-7
>
> Him we proclaim, warning everyone and teaching everyone with all wisdom, that we may present everyone mature in Christ. Colossians 1:28
>
> But the wisdom from above is first pure, then peaceable, gentle, open to reason, full of mercy and good fruits, impartial and sincere. James 3:17

It's so hard to know where to stop! The Bible is full of verses that show us how to become wise and where to find wisdom. These few are just the beginning to give you a taste for the topic.

Wisdom is in the Person of Jesus (Colossians 2:3), and we can lead our children into becoming wise through a plan. We should "touch the pallet" of our children with the Scriptures, and they should be able to see how much we love Jesus by how we actually live our daily life.

We can't guarantee our children will accept everything we attempt to teach them, but we can and must lead them to the Word of God. We should be having times of family devotion and prayer. Children should be included in the process of seeking God's will together as a family, especially in situations when they will be directly affected by the decision, such as decisions regarding moving, or changing churches, etc.

We should be people that read, quote, study and live out the Scriptures in our daily lives, and we should train our children to do the same as we are doing. No, we are not perfect, but we have a direction we are walking, and God expects us to take our children along that same path.

Remember Deuteronomy 6:4-9?

> "Hear, O Israel: The Lord our God, the Lord is one. You shall love the Lord your God with all your heart and with all your soul and with all your might. And these words that I command you today shall be on your heart. You shall teach them diligently to your children, and shall talk of them when you sit in your house, and when you walk by the way, and when you lie down, and when you rise. You shall bind them as a sign on your hand, and they shall be as frontlets between your eyes. You shall write them on the doorposts of your house and on your gates.

If we read this passage carefully and actually consider what it is saying, we can come to no other conclusion than God actually expects parents to teach their children the Word of God. Walking, sitting, getting up and going to sleep seems to cover just about all of the day!

Dangling them between our eyes and writing them on the doorposts, as well as the gate, certainly would keep the Scriptures fresh in our minds and homes. The point is not to actually do these things in the natural realm, but to dwell upon the Holy Word of God all the time and to make sure our children are trained to do so as well.

How do we achieve having wise young people? Start from birth to help them become familiar with the Scriptures. Give them a taste for the Word of God. Point out how the Bible gives practical answers to our every question. If you don't know how it does, then find out!

Children will catch what is important to you. If you go the Scriptures for answers, so will they. If you pray, so will they. If you make church attendance, giving, serving and having a daily time with the Lord important, so will your children. Children imitate what we do.

Remember Timothy, Paul's spiritual son? Perhaps Paul chose him because of this:

> But as for you, continue in what you have learned and have firmly believed, knowing from whom you learned it and how from childhood you have been acquainted with the sacred writings, which are able to make you wise for salvation through faith in Christ Jesus. 2 Timothy 3:14-15

Who taught Timothy these things?

> I am reminded of your sincere faith, a faith that dwelt first in your grandmother Lois and your mother Eunice and now, I am sure, dwells in you as well. 2 Timothy 1:5

God wants us to teach our children the Scripture, and this simple act will help move them along to maturity in all aspects of their lives.

So, after that somewhat long explanation about how to get wisdom, what does all that have to do with this chapter?

Foolishness is the natural default activity for children. It should not be so for young adults. As parents that want to end up with wise young adults, we must begin early to help our children grow in making wise choices.

We must challenge our children to understand the consequences of their behaviors and the motivations behind them. The proper perspective for comprehending both of these is given in the Word of God.

As we become more familiar with the wisdom given throughout our Bibles, we will learn to make better decisions. We will grow in faith and insight, and we will help our young people to become mature, which should be the desired result of all this training anyway!

Non-Rebellion Training:

If our goal is to have wise children, then we must teach them the basic principles of cause and effect. If you take this particular action then you will receive this particular result.

- Throw a baseball through a widow – pay for it with your own money.
- Keep forgetting to clean up your room – lose privileges on an increasing scale.
- Do the required task well – receive pay with even a bonus sometimes.
- Do the task poorly – receive a reduction in the reward.
- Show maturity in your words and actions – receive more freedom.
- Show immaturity in words and actions – receive more restrictions.

Training our children there are specific results to behavior and attitudes will help them learn to choose wisely. If we don't follow through here, we are doing them a disservice. When they move out into the world they will live in a cause and effect reality.

Bosses, police officers, teachers and judges do not excuse (at least they shouldn't) incorrect behavior; they give the appropriate reward or punishment for them.

While we do not spank for every infraction of our household rules, we should always be looking for teachable moments with an eye on the future growth and maturity of our children.

The reality is we will fall short and will not be perfect. However, knowing this reality does not change the direction we should be walking. We can't achieve perfection but we certainly can aim for consistency.

Discussion Thoughts:

1. How would you define the difference between rebellion and childishness?

2. Why do you think God gave us Wisdom literature in our Bibles? How does reading it help us become wise?

3. Why is it important for parents to teach their children cause and effect?

4. What are some examples of discipline other than spanking and when would you use them?

~~~~~~

Children should be trained in the way of benevolence and kindness to all…There is hardly an instruction relating to our duty more happily adapted to the capacity of children that that Golden Law- "Therefore all things whatsoever ye would that men should do to you, do ye even so them." – Matthew 7:12. This rule we should teach them and by this should examine their actions.

Philip Doddridge (1702-1751)
~~~~~~

11. Shooting Arrows

Like arrows in the hand of a warrior are the children of one's youth.
Psalm 127:4

The goal of all of this training is to release our children into their own lives. We all want wise, well-trained, mature young adults to go out into the world and live a life that matters for the Kingdom! That is a worthy goal.

Since we are not perfect, most of us will fall into one of two main ditches. We will release too soon, or we will try to hold on too long. Both are less than what we should be aiming for.

If we have done a good job in training our children and they have demonstrated mature thinking and decision making, the most rewarding thing we can do is send them out and enjoy the fruit of our labors.

John's famous passage is worth revisiting:

> I have no greater joy than to hear that my children are walking in the truth. 3 John 1:4

The satisfaction of knowing you have accomplished your job as a parent brings great joy to your heart and mind. When we can see the fruit of our labors, our heart smiles.

We will not see perfection, but we can see the results of our efforts. Our grown children will most likely marry and then produce their own children, and we will see even further proof of the fruit of our training.

This can be a scary time! It can also be a time of great joy and faith. God loves our children even more than we do. He will not fail and He will not forsake them. Go back and look at the chapter on God's promises if you feel faint and need encouragement!

We were not perfect parents, and we do not have perfect children. No one on this planet ever will, including you! You will fail and you will fall short. You will not be as consistent as you should have been. You will have demonstrated sinful behavior to your children, and you will realize that you didn't do all you should or could have. That is life.

We do the best we can and walk in faith. God has placed in the heart of most children the strong desire to love their parents regardless of their mistakes and failures. The same goes for parents towards their children. I understand there are exceptions, but in general terms, children can and will give a great deal of grace to their parents.

And, we all know that as we age, we realize our view and understanding change. We realize a lot of what we knew at sixteen or twenty has been enlarged, shaped, or rejected by the time we reach forty and beyond. In short, we grow up and we begin to understand the imperfect nature of our parents. Our children will do the same.

Releasing our Children:

We begin the process of releasing our children on our knees before the Throne of God. Most parents at some point or another have to give their children into the Lord's hands.

We love our children so very much that we can tend to get into a place of fear. We think we can do everything to protect them from anything they will face. We can't. We cannot live their lives. We cannot fight their battles. We cannot save them. We cannot choose for them and we cannot make their decisions forever. In fact, we damage them when we hold on too long.

The goal of training is to prepare and release them into the world.

At some point, and the sooner the better, we get on our knees and release our children into God's loving care. Some have called this "placing our children on the altar." We trust God to keep them, love them, protect them, and save them.

We also have to trust God that even if they die in this earthly life God is still good and still sovereign. He reigns over everything, and that includes over the lives of our children. While difficult, this battle must take place. Give your children to God and move to a place of faith as quickly as possible.

The next step we take in releasing our children begins with helping them to control their selfish, self-centered, "self-everything" lifestyle that they are born with until they are old enough to do so themselves.

These early days of battling the will issue are critical to helping our children learn how to live a life under authority. Everyone is under authority and the sooner we learn how to thrive there the better.

As we train our child in the behaviors we desire for them to learn, we are helping them get ready to fly out of our home. We want to train responsible young people that can be released and given into Kingdom service.

We pray over them and invest in them so they can leave and repeat the cycle with their children. This is how societies and nations survive. This principle is how the Kingdom of God expands on the earth. We call it discipleship, and it is best learned early and in the home.

As our children enter young adulthood we begin to test our training to see how it works out. We give small tasks releasing our controlling hands and see how the child performs. If they do well, we can expand the freedom. If they don't, then we figure out what additional training needs to be added. We test again and repeat until the desired results are achieved on a consistent basis.

In the business world a pattern is often used to train:

- I'll do the task and you watch me
- We will do the task together
- You do the task and I'll watch you

We can use this model in many areas of responsibility such as driving a car, running errands, and serving others. We let go, bring back in and process correcting anything that went wrong, and then repeat.

The goal is to have a successful launching of the arrows. We have them to shoot out, not to keep in our quiver. Arrows are used as an illustration of intent and action. Arrows are only successful if used, i.e. shot out and actually hit the target!

If we do a good job of training and have developed a relationship with our children, then when they leave the best is still ahead. Having adult children ask for your opinion and want you in their lives is a tremendous blessing.

If we invest in them while they are still under our roof they most often will want to continue that relationship long after they have their own roof.

Building a trusting, loving relationship takes a great deal of time and emotional energy, but it is well worth it. In fact, there is little else that will last a lifetime and bring such great joy to your life.

Helping your children navigate the perils of romance and finding a mate is a great honor. Being asked about major decisions long after the child has left the home is heart-warming and also brings a measure of contentment.

In addition, having a relationship with your children's children is a delight! A generational impact is possible if we invest in our children while they are young. We will never regret the amount of time we have spent, investing in our children, but many regret not doing so. We can't get the time back, so invest wisely now.

Focus on the Good:

On occasion we can become frustrated because our children are not perfect. We sometimes expect our children to act like they are fifty when they are fifteen. They won't. The only way to get to age fifty is to live fifty years. There are no shortcuts.

As caring parents we want our children to excel and grow way beyond where we are. This is commendable, but it takes time for our children to grow up. Remember how long it has taken you to reach where you are today? Whatever our level of maturity, we were not born with it; we lived out our lives day-by-day to get there. So will our children.

Our hope and prayer is that they will mature more quickly and become stronger than we are, and they should if we do a good job training them. However, it will still take time to get there, and we must allow time to pass. We must learn to give grace to both our children and to ourselves.

As parents it is easy to see everything that is going wrong with our children. All those quirks and issues they have scream out for us to correct them! Many of them are simply a reflection of either our training or what we have passed on to them, but still, we want to correct them as quickly and completely as possible.

We do not want our children to go through what we went through, so we will focus on what we don't like in their behavior or attitudes. This is good and necessary, but if we *only* focus here, it is very easy to miss the big picture.

We can become so absorbed in the 5-10% of our children's issues that we don't like we entirely miss the 90-95% of the good! This can dishearten a child and provoke them to frustration.

We can and must deal with the issues we see, but we also must focus on the good results that are there, or we will lead our children to believe that they can never please us or meet our expectations.

Perhaps that is one advantage of being a grandparent. When the grandchildren come over to the house it is easy to shut down whatever we are doing and simply enjoy them. We are not in the nitty gritty of daily training but enjoying the obvious fruit of that training. It is easier for one outside to see the results, while the one in the middle of the daily battles can struggle to see as clearly.

If possible, parents would be wise to step back a bit and see how well their children are really doing and not focus so much on the faults and imperfections. It is hard to do so, but I believe it would release some of the pressure if you can do it. No children are perfect, and expecting them to become perfect puts undue pressure on everyone.

Forgive me for using another example from the business world, but an old saying is helpful to consider – "aim at excellence not perfection." We can never achieve perfection, but we certainly can get to excellence with proper training and time investment. Enjoy the excellence and lay aside the impossible quest for perfection.

Future Spouses:

The previous principle would apply to a prospective spouse for your children as well. Most parents take the responsibility seriously about protecting their daughters when a young man comes calling. We should do the same with our sons, but guys typically do the calling so it's a bit different.

Whoever the young man is that eventually comes seeking the hand of your daughter he will most likely still be a young man. He will not be your age and he will not be as mature as you are. I know there are cases where an older man seeks a younger lady, but bear with me on this illustration.

We are typically 20-30 years more mature than our children. Some even 40 years older. Most young men that are prospective husbands and young ladies that are brides under consideration are going to be around the same age as our children, and so it should be.

Given this fact, why do we expect the young person to be as wise as we are, as financially well off, and as mature? They won't be. That doesn't mean they will not get there someday, but they most likely are not there yet. We must view prospective spouses with eyes of faith and not unrealistic evaluations of their current situation.

In most cases, marriage will help our children grow up and mature. As they begin to have their own children we will see the generational fruit of our labors and this will add even more joy to our lives.

Of course, our children will not adopt everything we attempted to train into them, but most will keep a great deal of it. Each partner in a marriage will help shape and adjust the other and we always pray and hope that they do so towards the good. Marriage is an excellent refining and growing tool, and we should want our children to embrace it when they are ready.

My warning here is for parents to lighten up a bit on the ones that come calling and those that are under consideration for marriage. Look for potential and direction, not perfection. Spouse selecting involves the heart and emotions, and many future relationship issues can be avoided if this process is walked out carefully and full of grace.

If you have developed a good relationship based on trust and open communication, then walking through the spouse selection process can be a wonderful time together. Parents should have helpful insights and so should siblings. A good working relationship will help in the choosing a life partner. (See appendix for an in-depth discussion on the topic of finding a spouse.)

Employment and Education:

These two topics always raise many questions. How, when, where, if needed, home, private, public, trade, apprenticeship? etc. There is no one-size-fits-all here just like training our children in all the other areas. Each one of our children was created in God's image and meant to accomplish good works for our Father:

> For we are his workmanship, created in Christ Jesus for good works, which God prepared beforehand, that we should walk in them. Ephesians 2:10

Every child should be trained to work at an early age. This can begin by simply emptying trash cans and picking up toys. Keeping a bedroom clean and helping with chores around the house should be a part of everyone's training. This basic process lays the groundwork for a good work ethic.

When children reach an age of maturity more duties can and should be assigned. Every child can and should become a good worker. Depending on the goals for the child, an outside-of-the-home job can be undertaken, thus helping to develop maturity and an appreciation for life as an adult.

Maturity and influences need to be considered in both education and employment decisions. "How strong is the faith of the young person?" and "Are they ready to resist the onslaught of peer pressure, temptation and verbal abuse that will probably follow a godly young person?" are good questions to consider.

If the young adult is attempting to live a life of godliness, they will incur abuse as promised by Jesus:

> Indeed, all who desire to live a godly life in Christ Jesus will be persecuted… 2 Timothy 3:12

A young man or woman who takes a stand for moral purity, perhaps against abortion or a perverted lifestyle, will probably be verbally attacked. Are they ready to withstand it? Have they been trained to respond in love and kindness to the onslaught? Do your children understand what they believe and why they believe it?

There are multiple resources available to answer the questions regarding education and employment choices, so I won't develop them here. If you want to see what I have written about these subjects see – *Gospel Legacy – A Church and Family Model Reaching Beyond our Generation.* There is also an article on school choices in the Appendix for your reading pleasure.

There are many more issues to consider in releasing our arrows into a dark world. For now, the primary questions to consider are how prepared are they and how much light do they have to share? How strong of a belief system and foundation do they have? Are they ready to give an answer to the questions that will be asked as the Apostle Peter advises here:

> But even if you should suffer for righteousness' sake, you will be blessed. Have no fear of them, nor be troubled, but in your hearts honor Christ the Lord as holy, always being prepared to make a defense to anyone who asks you for a reason for the

> hope that is in you; yet do it with gentleness and respect, having a good conscience, so that, when you are slandered, those who revile your good behavior in Christ may be put to shame.
> 1 Peter 3:14-16

Begin to explain to your children what you believe and, as they age, why you believe it. Make sure they grasp the reasons behind the behavioral choices you have made. Allow time for questions and discussion as the child matures.

Begin to expose them to some challenging situations and explain how to deal with it. Be sure to have them grounded in the Word of God and help them learn how to seek answers to their questions.

There is no perfect formula, and there is not a perfect approach to discipleship of our children. Each one is a unique gift from our Father, and He expects us to appreciate them and to train them in His ways and thoughts. We must learn what God expects first, then pass what we have discovered along to those we will send out of our homes.

There are additional resources in the appendix section of this book to help with the discipleship process. Take heart! You can do this for the Lord is with you!

Discussion Thoughts:

1. Why do you think arrows are used as an example for children?

2. What do you think John meant when he said he had no greater joy than to know his children walked in the truth?

3. Why do you think God created the parent child relationship the way He did (for He certainly could have done it differently)?

4. How do you intend to train your children to face the realities of a world dominated by sin and darkness?

12. Failures, Foolish Choices, Grace

Give instruction to a wise man, and he will be still wiser; teach a righteous man, and he will increase in learning. Proverbs 9:9

The Apostle John said he had no greater joy than to know his children walked in the truth, but the opposite is also true. There is no greater heartache than to have adult children reject their parents' faith.

With just about every major study showing a large number of young people leaving the faith, it can be a fearful thing to enter parenthood. We can tend to think, "Why bother if all my children are simply going to walk away and reject everything I taught them?"

The short answer is we are commanded in God's Word to train our children, therefore we have a commission from our Lord to do so. It is not an option for us to disobey. Okay, I know we can, but it should not be!

The longer answer is that we must reach a place of faith and trust in the goodness of our Sovereign God. We know the Scriptures are true, and we covered many of God's promises earlier regarding our children and their future. We do our part and God does His.

God will, of course, do it much better than we, perfectly, in fact. We will fail and often fall short, but we must get up and keep on working. God is not shocked by our failures nor frustrated over them. Not if He really is Sovereign!

Fear of failing can paralyze us into inactivity and even disobedience to God's clear commands to train our children. We must not go down that path. We do our best because God expects us to do so.

God will give us the grace necessary to stand, or get back up, but we must continue with the job we have been given until we are finished. We learn how to wait upon the Lord, renew our strength, and then get back out there soaring like an eagle (Isaiah 40:31).

I know sometimes it feels more like crawling with the bugs than soaring with the majestic birds, but we simply don't have the proper perspective; God does.

God is the only One that has all of the information, and He alone knows exactly what is really going on. Our view is cloudy, at best, and often distorted with sin, fear, doubt, worry, etc. God's view never is! God is faithful, just, and true. His Word never fails and He will never, ever, ever forsake us, nor our children. Therefore, we walk on with His empowering grace doing the best we can.

For Those That Have Failed:

Perhaps you are reading this and your children are already grown and out of the home. Maybe they didn't turn out like you dreamed or desired. After reading this far, perhaps you have come to the conclusion that you failed in some way, or even in many ways. Don't despair!

Our God is good, faithful, just, loving, and He lavishes His grace upon us (see Ephesians 1:7-8). God loves our children, including yours and mine! God is not finished with any of us yet.

If we have seen some failures in our life, this is a good thing. None of us is perfect, and all of us are in varying degrees of growth. This also implies we are in varying degrees of failure. When we see a failure in our life, we run into the arms of mercy and find help in our time of need.

Consider just a few passages to find comfort from Love Himself:

> If we confess our sins, he is faithful and just to forgive us our sins and to cleanse us from all unrighteousness. 1 John 1:9

> Come to me, all who labor and are heavy laden, and I will give you rest. Matthew 11:28

> All that the Father gives me will come to me, and whoever comes to me I will never cast out. John 6:37

> Keep your life free from love of money, and be content with what you have, for he has said, "I will never leave you nor forsake you." Hebrews 13:5 (quoting Deuteronomy 31:6)

> In that day you will ask in my name, and I do not say to you that I will ask the Father on your behalf; for the Father himself loves you, because you have loved me and have believed that I came from God. John 16:26-27

There are hundreds of other verses that deal with God's love for us and His forgiveness of our sins and how we are now viewed through His eyes. We are His dearly loved children and He will never reject us because we failed. He loves us.

If God has brought some failure to your mind and you have seen the impact of that issue, then attempt to deal with it. Go to the child or spouse that was the recipient of your actions and ask for forgiveness. Even if they refuse to offer forgiveness, you have done your part by asking. God forgives you completely because He sees us through the blood of Jesus.

One important note about asking for forgiveness is this: confess specifically. Many attempt to ask for forgiveness by saying something like, "I am sorry you are upset," or, "It's clear you are angry, so please forgive me." These types of apologies typically make the person even more angry.

It is far better to take the blame for your actions. Say something like, "I know I promised you we would go to the zoo, and I didn't keep that promise. I know that hurt you when I acted that way, so would you please forgive me for my behavior?"

Do you see the difference between the two apologies? The first one is actually blaming the other person, and the second one is taking responsibility for personal actions. Which one do you think will have a greater impact?

The Scripture states in Romans 12:18 – "If possible, so far as it depends on you, live peaceably with all." We must do our part and then leave the rest up to the Holy Spirit. Sometimes it will take a while for a wounded child or spouse to forgive. Maybe it will even take all the way to heaven before it happens. We have no control over the response but a great deal of control over our words and actions.

Foolish Choices:

Even with the best parental training, children can make foolish choices. Remember Adam and Eve? God the Father was perfect yet His first kids chose foolishly.

The goal of this book is to help us train our children. With that backdrop in view, if they go astray, they are making a willful choice to reject what we have taught them and not making that choice from a lack of information.

We are responsible for what we do and how we do it. We are not held accountable for how others respond, or whether or not they reject, or ignore our teaching. Our job is to train and teach. The one under that training and teaching will have to decide how they accept it and how much of it they keep.

Our children can and will make foolish choices, just like you and I have done. Our goal and hope is they will not make the same ones we made. We pray and hope our teaching will help them on their journey of life and avoid the holes we fell into.

We won't do a perfect job and neither will they. We cannot expect perfection from our children any more than we can expect perfection from ourselves.

With that said, we can help inform our children of the consequences of choices and also share what we have learned by our own mistakes. Nothing is wasted in the Kingdom of God, including our failures. They can always serve as an example to be avoided!

We can also try to help our children avoid making foolish choices by training them to discern good from evil. We can limit what we give them a "taste" for as described earlier in the book.

Many times parents approach me and ask "Where did we go wrong?"" when their young person is heading the wrong direction in attitude or actions.

While not the complete answer, I encourage parents to look at the following influences:

- Who are the friends of your children? The Scriptures state: "Whoever walks with the wise becomes wise, but the companion of fools will suffer harm." Proverbs 13:20
- What type of music is the young person feeding their soul upon? Every artist has a purpose for their work, and this includes music. Know well who is impacting your child's

mind with music, for it has proven to be the downfall of many.

- In our day, we must add social media and the influence of easy access to the internet. What is your young person feeding upon in the vastness of easy access to pornography and sensual stimuli online?

It is hard to limit or protect our children from everything, but we must use wisdom in what we expose them to and how early we allow them the complete freedom to make those choices. Hours and hours of unsupervised television, internet, or games can certainly add to the process of making poor choices. We are told to know well the condition of our flocks (Proverbs 27:23), and we should know what they are feasting upon in their souls.

As our children age, we must explain why certain choices are harmful. We should detail why we don't like a particular song or movie choice. Generationally speaking there will always be a difference in preferential choices, but sin, carnality, crude, sexual in nature, etc. type behaviors are never beneficial.

We want to help train wise children that can grow into productive, servant-oriented young people who develop into desirable marriage partners or strong, stable single servants in the Kingdom. This rarely happens by chance, but often does with a plan and vision.

The best way to overcome foolish choices is to avoid them in the first place. I have often asked a question that I believe is worth considering:

Is it better to overcome temptation or to avoid it in the first place?

While your answer may vary depending on the circumstances, I have found that we rarely make good choices when we are in the heat of the moment or unprepared for the battle. We must help our children learn to think through their decisions *before* they are faced with them, at least in principle if not specifics.

How will they make the right choice when sexual temptation shows up? Or, when lying will get them out of punishment? Or when cheating on a test will get them praise or a better grade? Or when no one will ever know if I look at that website or steal that candy bar, etc.?

Helping our children grow in wisdom and character will go a long way in helping avoid foolish choices as they grow up.

Grace:

Grace is a word that is both wonderful and abused. Grace is used as an excuse for sin and for just about every carnal decision made. "I'm under grace" is used as a license for sin and for justification for almost anything I want to do.

Grace is also God's wonderful outpouring upon His children. He lavishes it upon us (Ephesians 1:8), and for that I am eternally grateful.

We experience saving grace, empowering grace, and amazing grace. I love grace! I'm all for grace, and I pray for even more grace as I walk through this life. I pray for grace for my wife, children, church and just about everybody I know. Who could ever get too much grace?

So, we as parents must learn how to walk in grace towards our children and towards ourselves. Our children will make mistakes and so will each one of us. We need grace in our homes and lots of it!

We need grace to forgive and grace to endure. We need grace to grow in patience and grace to take a stand and do what is right. We need to teach our children to give grace to others and also to themselves. We need grace.

We need to teach our children how to forgive others and how to deal with guilt. We need to teach them how to walk in love towards others and how to love the Lord with all their heart, soul, mind, and strength.

In case you haven't noticed it yet, I love grace. I don't however, love abusing the term, and I am in good company in both respects.

> For you were called to freedom, brothers. Only do not use your freedom as an opportunity for the flesh, but through love serve one another. Galatians 5:13

> Live as people who are free, not using your freedom as a cover-up for evil, but living as servants of God. 1 Peter 2:16

These two spiritual heavyweights dealt with the same issue – don't use grace as a cover up for sin or a license for carnality. We are under grace, but grace is given so we can learn how to love and serve others. Grace is never given so we can sin or justify selfish behavior or the fulfilling of our fleshly desires.

We all need to embrace the gift of grace given from our loving Father. We need to learn how to extend grace to others when they hurt us or let us down. We need to teach our children how to walk in grace, and we begin by modeling it for them.

As we discipline them we do it in grace. As we correct improper actions and attitudes we do it in grace. We don't excuse sinful behavior under the banner of grace, we walk in grace as we deal with it – just like God does for us. God lavishes His grace upon us even while He is dealing with us as His children:

> But when we are judged by the Lord, we are disciplined so that we may not be condemned along with the world.
> 1 Corinthians 11:32

> And have you forgotten the exhortation that addresses you as sons? "My son, do not regard lightly the discipline of the Lord, nor be weary when reproved by him. For the Lord disciplines the one he loves, and chastises every son whom he receives."
> Hebrews 12:5-6

> It is for discipline that you have to endure. God is treating you as sons. For what son is there whom his father does not discipline? If you are left without discipline, in which all have participated, then you are illegitimate children and not sons.
> Hebrews 12:7-8

> For they disciplined us for a short time as it seemed best to them, but he disciplines us for our good, that we may share his holiness. For the moment all discipline seems painful rather than pleasant, but later it yields the peaceful fruit of righteousness to those who have been trained by it.
> Hebrews 12:10-11

> Those whom I love, I reprove and discipline, so be zealous and repent. Revelation 3:19

God lavishes His grace, and He disciplines us because He loves us perfectly. He has instructed us to do the same with our children as we attempt to train them in the way they should go. We are not perfect like our Father in heaven, but we rely upon His grace to help us make a greater amount of better decisions than poor ones.

I have had many people respond to me when complimented on some behavior, skill, or in reference to their children with a comment like, "it's all by God's grace."

I understand what they mean, but allow me just a few words to express how incomplete that thought is. If someone would tell an Olympic swimmer or a professional athlete that their skills and accomplishments are all by grace, do you think that would be accurate?

The natural, and also quite true, reply could be, "Well it may be grace, but the thousands of hours I put in the gym might have something to do with it also!"

Having played competitive racquetball for many, many years, I learned several skills that were developed by repeated usage and training. Practice, correcting improper techniques, investing time in watching those better at the game, etc. all went into become a better player.

I could say, "yup, it's all by grace,' but that would only be a part of the story. Yes, it is by God's grace that I can run, see, and hit a fast moving ball. However, the hundreds of hours of work are also involved.

I have played many guys that were stronger, bigger, faster, and younger than me and beat them by a huge margin. The difference was not grace, but the work I had put in before playing them.

I have known many parents that did an excellent job raising their children, and in a spirit of humility they will say, "It's all grace." I gently remind them that the thousands of hours they put in worked right alongside God's grace to produce an excellent product!

If it simply is by God's grace, then why bother? Why invest the time and energy to train, stay up late talking, praying and crying over our children? Just relax, it's all grace. We know this simply is not true or God would not have commanded us to invest all the time and effort into the job of parenting.

Yes, it takes God's grace to make it, and He of course works through the Holy Spirit minute by minute to lead and guide us.

It also takes a huge amount of time and energy to invest in the next generation.

From sleepless nights with newborns, to schooling choices and activities, to navigating the boy-girl relationships until marriage, thousands of hours are invested by concerned parents. God gives us the grace to go on, but we invest the time and training in our children.

If it simply is God's grace and our impact makes no difference, then we certainly can't be held responsible for anything wrong in our children. We can't be held responsible for anything right either. It just happened by some accident. God gave grace to this family, and then He must not have to the other one where the children have been all messed up in drugs, suffered abuse or perhaps ended up in jail.

Over the decades of working with parents, it seems clear to me that God's grace works better in conjunction with active parents than with the uninvolved. The parents that supervise and oversee tend to experience more grace than those that allow their children to run wild, I guess. Or, is it a partnership between God's grace and the parents' efforts?

Summary:

One day, the senior pastor I served under for eleven years ran off with his book editor to Florida. The church was devasted and many lives were thrown into turmoil. He was over fifty years old at the time. So, was it his parents fault that he ran off into sexual immorality?

How about if the pastor had been forty? Thirty? Twenty? Where do we draw the line between the individual actions of the person and the lack of proper training from the parents?

Many parents struggle with guilt when their adult children sin. They feel as if they had done something different those sinful choices would not have been made. This is a trap and a waste of emotional energy.

God, Who is perfect, experienced His children choose sin. Was it poor parenting or free will? Adam and Even knew what God had said and chose to disobey His direct command. So, was it God's fault or theirs?

I don't know the exact answer to the question of when and where to draw the line regarding age, but I do know that every adult can choose to sin. I also know that if and when they do choose to sin, the parents are not to blame. The choice made is the responsibility of the one making it.

Every parent other than God has made mistakes. Every one of us can look back over our lives and see things we could have and perhaps should have done differently. That does not mean we are at fault when our grown children choose poorly - they are.

We do our best as parents and we train and invest in the next generation. We teach our children the right and wrongs of life, but when they leave our homes, they begin a new one. Our job of direct, hands-on parenting goes away and, hopefully, we become sought after counselors.

Our responsibility regarding the adult child's decisions also goes away. They are now free to choose how they will live and what they will do.

As previously stated, there are not grandchildren in the Kingdom of God, only children. Each member of God's family comes in through the Door of Jesus and is adopted into the Family under the authority of the King. God becomes their Father and the Holy Spirit becomes their guide.

Parents of adult children are now in the role of advisor, counselor and hopefully friend. As children leave the homes of their parents, the responsibility for their actions leaves with them. We grow to trust that God is their Father and He will do the job well!

Discussion Thoughts:

1. How would you explain grace and its role in parenting?

2. How does the choice of friends impact a child or young person?

3. Why do you think God chose the family model to reveal Himself to us, including the discipline aspects addressed in Hebrews 12?

4. How would explain the tension between grace and work involved in parenting

13. Hope for Generations

And his mercy is for those who fear him from generation to generation.
Luke 1:50

By just about any standard of evaluation the coming generations are in real trouble. Whether it is crime statistics or surveys of religious understanding, it is a fearful time to be a parent.

This was true for previous generations as well, but we don't live then, we live now. Like previous generations, our only hope is in the Lord. It must be. We live by faith, not fear, and we must parent in the same fashion.

> For this reason I remind you to fan into flame the gift of God, which is in you through the laying on of my hands, for God gave us a spirit not of fear but of power and love and self-control. 2 Timothy 1:6-7

> Have I not commanded you? Be strong and courageous. Do not be frightened, and do not be dismayed, for the Lord your God is with you wherever you go. Joshua 1:9

If God is for us, then what do we need to be afraid of? If God is on our side, and He is, then we can get up each day and boldly walk through it meeting it head on. I know, some days we just want to stay under the covers and not face the day, but we must! We will make a choice on how we face it, so let's choose hope and faith.

This generation of parents is facing some very difficult situations. Some are new, like the proliferation of pornography over the internet and the flagrant disregard of any moral restraints. Though, it could be argued the latter has existed almost since the beginning of creation. Remember Sodom and Gomorrah? What was their issue again?

The push from media, educators and the humanist system to remove God from schools and turn any moral view into hate speech, is also both new and old. God's people have always stood out as different from the nations around Her. The problem came when She embraced those views instead of walking in God's ways.

Today, the far fringe of society has demanded and succeeded in moving aberrant behavior into the acceptable range. All manner of perverseness is put forward as normal, and only Christian morality is allowed to be mocked and rejected. Parents will have to figure out how to help their young people navigate in such a world.

Again, this is not all that new, for the Romans and Greeks both worshiped the naked body and actively promoted all manner of sexual deviancy. As believers, we must learn how to walk in love towards the unlovely and to be light in a dark world.

Darkness will always give way to light, so we must learn how to raise wise children to further the Gospel message to a world lost in sin and death. This goal has not changed from the beginning.

With the destruction of the nuclear family, young adults coming from a two-parent home gain an advantage. Studies have always shown children growing up in an intact home do far better in school, on the job, and in their own marriages than those is a single or no parent type home.

This is not meant to hurt or belittle those that have suffered through the pain of divorce and are now struggling to raise a child or children alone. Each of the single parents I know would readily share how much harder it is alone and how much better it would be for there to be a unified two rather than a divided one raising the children. God gives additional grace to children and parents in these difficult situations.

My point is that we must take advantage of the blessing of having two parents in the home to train the children. If we do, the children will stand out in the workforce and can take on leadership roles that others can't or often are not equipped to do so.

We have wandered away from the Scriptures and from faith as a nation that was founded as "one under God." The answer, at least in part, rests in turning around and walking back towards both God and the Bible.

If we keep doing the same things we have been doing, we will not get different results. And we know, that this is one definition of being insane when we expect different results without changing anything! We must change, and we must return to God's instructions if we hope to make a difference in our world.

If we do, then we can expect God to pour out His promised blessings and move upon our family and nation. We typically think about this passage during a specific time of repentance for our nation, but doesn't it apply for our families as well?

> If my people who are called by my name humble themselves, and pray and seek my face and turn from their wicked ways, then I will hear from heaven and will forgive their sin and heal their land. 2 Chronicles 7:14

Many Christians have rejected God's clear commands already written in this book to train their children. Is one definition of "wicked ways" not doing what God has so clearly instructed? In fact, isn't that disobedience? What would happen if every family we knew actually began to disciple their own children and took the Scriptures I have shared in this book seriously?

I believe that a generation of strong young men and women would be released into a dark and dying world and change would begin. Service and evangelism would spread, and change would come as the God who hears from heaven forgives sin and heals lands.

No matter how far a culture has dropped into depravity, light and life will overcome. We must learn to love those that are lost in sin and death, but we do not, nor should we imitate their behaviors.

We must learn how to train the generation we are responsible for to take stands upon God's Holy Word and for the advancement of His Kingdom in this world.

We are ambassadors for Christ and each home that names His name is now an outpost for righteousness in a dark and weary land.

We unite with others that have a similar vision and we do our best to raise sharp arrows.

As we grow in our walk with the Lord, we know we can't do everything that needs to be accomplished, but we can and must do what we are able to do. This certainly would include training those under our direct influence wouldn't it? As the world around us continues to grow darker, the light within our own lives will shine even brighter. Our marriages and our family will provide an opportunity to share the glorious Gospel with a lost and dying world.

The Light has always been offensive to the darkness, but it also has been attractive to those hungry for a new way of living. Under persecution and rejection, the Gospel thrives! It will be the same in our day and in the days of our children.

We are called to make disciples by our Lord's final command in Matthew 28:18-20, and my appeal to you is to begin in your own home.

The disciples of Jesus turned the perverted Roman empire upside down, and the disciples we make can and will do the same in our desperate world.

Don't give up and don't give in! Keep on praying, seeking and training the next generation, for the Good News of Jesus is still needing to be heard and seen until He returns.

Discussion Thoughts:

1. As a parent are you full of fear or faith as you consider the role you have been given?

2. How does home discipleship help spread the Gospel?

3. Is there anything that you have read in this book that revealed a need for change in your parenting?

4. What will you do now with what you have read?

~~~~~~

Many are careful to educate their children in the favor of great men, but, alas! who brings up his children in the fear of the great God?

George Swinnock (1627-1673)
~~~~~~

Part Two – For Further Study

Part Two includes some articles and studies to further assist you in seeking to do the best job you possible can in your parenting duties assigned by God. You certainly do not have to agree with me on all the topics covered, but they are provided to stimulate thinking and conversation.

Be the Resource for Your Children as they Mature

I have often said that the difference between a child that excels and avoids trouble, and one that fails, is one main thing—parental supervision. While this is not the only ingredient, it is a key one. Parents must know what their children are thinking and doing.

> The rod and reproof give wisdom, but a child left to himself brings shame to his mother. (Proverbs 29:15)

> Know well the condition of your flocks, and give attention to your herds. (Proverbs 27:23)

My wife and I used to have a small flock of goats. Well, in fact, we had two – goats that is. One day I went up to the barn and saw one of the goats had managed to become trapped in the area where we kept a hay bale for their eating pleasure. Her front leg was stuck, and she was screaming up a storm.

As I helped her out, I wondered how long she had been in that twisted position. She could not help herself, and her sister certainly did not tell me. How long she was stuck I will never know, but I do know that the only way I found out was to go up to the barn!

As parents, we are given a flock to shepherd. It may be small or large, but God expects us to take care of it for Him! At least part of that responsibility is to know what the little lambs are doing, and with whom they are doing it.

How do you know that your children are acting as you wish if you are not observing their behavior and conversation? How do you know they are being kind or sharing if you cannot see or hear them? "I do not need to watch them because they are with good kids," protests the parent to me. How do you know they are good kids? Do you know how long it takes a good kid to become something less than good?

While it may vary as to length of time, Proverbs states a child left alone will eventually bring shame. How do you know if their legs are not stuck somewhere they ought not to be if you do not check on them? They could be crying for hours, and their brothers or sisters may not tell you. Severe damage can happen quickly, so we must be aware.

Parents must check on the flocks under their care, and they must do so often.

One of the young men in my church invited me to begin using Facebook. I agreed and ventured out into the world of cyberspace as part of my responsibility as pastor to "know well the condition of my flock." It has been both enjoyable and enlightening.

I have since challenged the parents in my church to go out and visit their children's pages. Do they know who their children's friends are? Do they know what personal information is being revealed and talked about, for the whole cyber world to see? Do they know the pictures that are out there, or the music groups their children love? If not, why not? Do the parents know who the children are texting or talking with in the multiple chat rooms that are available? Parents should know so they can assist their children to make godly decisions.

Of course, it takes time; shepherding is a time-consuming occupation. Parents often ask me in the midst of a crisis, "Where did I go wrong?" My response often is, "You let go too early." About the time that parents should be more involved, they are taking their hands off and giving away too much freedom to children not ready for it.

We would not dream of letting our children drive our brand new cars without instruction and supervision, but we let them navigate the Internet and make potentially dangerous friendships, often allowing them to become emotionally and even physically involved with the opposite sex long before they are trained.

Many debate over the age when parents should let go, and I will not settle the debate here. A helpful principle is that as the child demonstrates maturity and the ability to handle freedom, the parent can give more freedom. Some children are mature beyond their years and others are not; a wise parent will know the difference.

As far as I can tell, the Bible does not provide a specific age. Eighteen and twenty-one are ages that our society has deemed as sufficient, but scripturally, there are no such arbitrary lines. I prefer to deal with the concept of being under a parent's authority rather than an age seemingly randomly selected by our secular society.

Ideally, a daughter will be able to remain under her father's authority until her daddy walks her down the aisle to her waiting groom on their wedding day. The same would be true for a son, except that he is the recipient, being given the bride by another father! Some will marry younger than others will, but that should be the parent's decision, and not based on some random age picked out of thin air. As a child matures and demonstrates the ability to act responsibly, more freedom can and should be given.

Boy/Girl Relationships

It is perfectly natural for girls to be attracted to boys and boys to girls. This process begins somewhat earlier with the girls, but boys catch up soon enough. As our children moved through adolescence, we had many open and honest conversations about these normal desires and drives. If the parents do not discuss such things, where will the children get their information? From the government schools? The Internet? Friends that are the same age? TV or movies? Parents are the best, and, I believe, the God-chosen resource to help their children grow and understand the sexual arena. This may be a stretch for some parents, but it is well worth the effort and discomfort you may experience to ensure your children are well prepared to face the hormonal battle that will soon be upon them.

God designed the attraction between male and female, and parents are the proper resource to explain how best to channel that attraction until it can be righteously fulfilled. Boys need to be careful about stirring up emotions in girls, and girls need to be aware of how they dress their temple of the Holy Spirit.

One of my daughters is very affectionate and loves to hug and touch people as a sign of affection. We had to explain to her that touching a young man's knee might not mean the same thing to her as it does to him, especially if he is lovesick! She needed to guard herself around young men and be aware of what she was doing in order to protect them. This same daughter wanted to wear a miniskirt. We asked her why she wanted to wear one and her reply was interesting. "The guys are all attracted to the girls that show more skin, and I want them to like me, too," was her explanation.

We could not deny the fact the young men did follow the young ladies around who were dressed in that way, but we encouraged our daughter to check her heart motives. "Is that really the type of man you want to marry? Do you want to chuck your values simply to get some guy to ogle over you?" Many such questions were asked and multiple conversations followed. She eventually saw our logic and agreed that it was more important to please God and her parents than some young man that she most likely would not end up marrying. For the record, I would not have allowed her to wear the skirt outside of her bedroom anyway, but I was more concerned about her motives than the clothing.

Underneath our choices rest multiple motives and we must understand and deal with these motives. Simply putting a bunch of rules in place without understanding motives can lead to legalism.

In my opinion, many parents allow their children to become involved with the opposite sex excessively early. Relationships can become very passionate and emotionally binding at a young age, while, realistically, neither party is ready or able to marry. We attempted to acknowledge the attraction our children may have developed toward someone, acknowledging it was part of the normal developmental process, and then began to discuss what to do with it.

When children are pre-teen or early- to mid-teen, they cannot marry, and encouraging them in relationships with someone is setting them up for heartache and potential disaster. Parents need to be aware of what their sons or daughters are thinking, and with whom they are involved, even if only in their minds.

Children need their parents to help them process the confusing emotions they will inevitably face. We attempted to avoid the sexual problems associated with traditional dating by encouraging our children to wait until they were old enough to consider marriage before becoming involved in relationships. Dating and going steady often prepare someone better for divorce than for a life-long marital commitment. I believe it is wiser to wait until it can be righteously fulfilled before awakening love and sexual desire in our young people.

As a pastor, I do a significant amount of pre-marriage counseling and most young couples struggle with sexual desire for their soon-to-be spouses. This is natural and increases as the honeymoon approaches. The young people who have drawn clear lines on physical touching, and have practiced parental inclusion, are usually successful. The ones who do not protect themselves through parental involvement, and do not have clear lines drawn regarding physical contact, usually fail morally.

What are your children watching in their rooms or listening to on those earbuds? Who is your child e-mailing or texting? When they go out at night, do you know where they are going, and with whom they are spending time? Do you have access to your child's e-mail account or cell phone records? Do you know what websites your child has visited lately? Some may call this snooping; I call it being involved.

If your child is resistant to your knowing, shouldn't that bother you? What is there to hide anyway? Typically, things done under the cover of darkness and secrecy bring death and destruction. If your child were viewing pornography already, wouldn't it be better to help him or her get over it now, instead of waiting until it is an addiction? Parents must be involved and active in order to assist their children in developing the necessary skills to survive in this lust-crazed world. The training must begin when children are young and be consistently applied as long as they are under their parents' roofs.

Even with patient, consistent instruction, children can still make foolish choices; after they have grown up and left your home, however, they would be choosing against what they know, instead of simply making an uninformed choice. We must give our children a fighting chance to make it in this world, and it begins almost from the day they are born!

Time, Modesty and Lust

"Well, I agree with some of what you just wrote, but it sounds like it will take a lot of time," you may be thinking. You are absolutely correct! Talking, the willingness to interfere, confrontation, the challenging of incorrect assumptions and what I call "intense fellowship," are all part of an involved parent's tasks.

No one ever said parenting was easy. To be effective, it involves a great deal of self-sacrifice and time on the parent's part. The training of their children has been delegated to parents from the very hand of God, and we must be willing to invest ourselves completely in the task (See Deuteronomy 6).

In the scripture, children are referred to as "gifts," and "fruit," and we must take care of them with all diligence. Investing time in our children will not guarantee they will never fail, but if they do fall, it will not be because we did not attempt to train them. Our efforts can help them get ready for the world they will face as they leave our home. We must prepare them. If we do not, who will?

Parents need to help their children understand from a young age what lust (See my book *Courage to Flee* if you don't know what this is) is and how to defeat it. We need to teach our sons the law of first glance, and train our daughters the proper way to handle their bodies around men.

We need to instruct them about the proper role of sex inside of marriage, and not let them be trained by Hollywood or the Internet.

As our children move into puberty, parents should be the ones discussing what is occurring in them physically, emotionally, and spiritually. The task should not be left to some perverted producer of pornography or some other humanistic purveyor. Our sons will be exposed to an almost constant barrage of sensuality; are they ready? Will our daughters be part of the problem, or will they be part of a group that helps raise up a new standard of modesty and decency?

I sometimes marvel at fathers and husbands and wonder if they have forgotten what it is like to be male. Perhaps it is more complicated than that-- maybe they are fearful of confrontation, but allowing their wives or daughters to dress sensually is foolish at best, and opening the door for immorality at worst.

I wonder why some men do not look at their wives or daughters and place themselves in the mindset of other men. Do you really want other men's eyes drawn to your wives' or daughters' cleavage, or skintight clothes highlighting their chests or rear ends? Are you secretly proud of how they look, perhaps wanting to show them off, and encouraging them to wear clothing that is excessively tight?

If that is true, or even partially true, what kind of motive is that? Have you forgotten the struggles you have with someone else's wife or daughter? Perhaps it would be beneficial to take another look at what we allow or encourage and recheck our motives. Is purity our goal, or sensuality or pride? Are we comparing our styles and actions to the world's system or to God's Word? Are we adding to the degradation of our culture or attempting to present a higher standard? Only you can answer these questions for yourself, but your family desperately needs you to do it! The church needs you to do it, and our society needs you to take a second look and make sure holiness and modesty are the goals.

Change come slowly, but perhaps they would take place more quickly if each family addressed these issues in addition to the organized church doing so. If we addressed these issues, we would present a very clear difference to the world around us. Based on what is currently popular, there is very little difference between the Christians and the world. I hear men and women of God, both young and old, saying to and about each other, "You look hot!" or, "That is such a hot dress." I wonder if the people who are saying such things are actually aware of what they sound like. Is the goal of a godly woman to be "hot"? What does that mean anyway? In my BC days (Before Christ), we used a numbering system of sorts, with ten being the best looking, and one being on the other end of the scale. What were we evaluating? The scale was really a lust meter, and Christians have adopted it! When a husband tells his wife that she looks "hot" in the privacy of their home, that is one thing, but does he really want other men looking at what he alone is allowed to enjoy? The same would hold true with our daughters.

Have we adopted the world's system of lust and embraced it so much that we do not even think about it anymore? Is there any connection between these issues and the skyrocketing divorce rate of Christians? What do we stir up in our wives if we encourage them to be seductive? What will happen if a wife is "hot" and ends up running off with some other man who enjoyed her "hotness"? Will we then be glad that we promoted this philosophy?

What about the well-documented fact that the vast majority of young people cast off their parents' faith, and many end up in immorality, shortly after they leave the home? Are there any connections? We must find the answer as parents if the Church and family are to survive. We must be willing to go before the throne of the King and ask His opinion of such matters. I already know some of God's views on such topics. Carefully consider the following verses and think about what our sensual world system promotes, and if we as believers in Jesus Christ should imitate that philosophy:

> Do not be conformed to this world, but be transformed by the renewal of your mind, that by testing you may discern what is the will of God, what is good and acceptable and perfect. Romans 12:2

> Now we have received not the spirit of the world, but the Spirit who is from God, that we might understand the things freely given us by God. 1 Corinthians 2:12

> You adulterous people! Do you not know that friendship with the world is enmity with God? Therefore whoever wishes to be a friend of the world makes himself an enemy of God. James 4:4

> Do not love the world or the things in the world. If anyone loves the world, the love of the Father is not in him. For all that is in the world—the desires of the flesh and the desires of the eyes and pride in possessions—is not from the Father but is from the world. 1 John 2:15–16

> Beloved, do not imitate evil but imitate good. Whoever does good is from God; whoever does evil has not seen God. (3 John 1:11)

We need to evaluate seriously our standards and desires in light of these verses. The world system stands in direct opposition to the Kingdom of God, and we must be careful not to imitate our enemy. We must train our children to recognize the world system and how it wants to dilute the Christian message. We can only serve one Lord, and it must be Jesus! We as parents must be involved with the lives of our children and help them navigate in the sexual realm. If you have been on the sidelines, it is time to get involved. Many have fallen into bondage and more will join them in our lifetime. Maybe you are one of them. One passage that constantly gives me hope is:

> At one time we too were foolish, disobedient, deceived and enslaved by all kinds of passions and pleasures. We lived in malice and envy, being hated and hating one another. Titus 3:3

The "at one time" means they were no longer living for those things and the same should be true for all believers. What are we living for? What are our children doing right now?

~~~~~~

It is not enough that we pray as private individuals in our closets; we are required to honor God in our families as well.
Arthur W. Pink (1886-1952)
~~~~~~

Practical Family Discipleship Tools

Every follower of Christ is called to make disciples as part of the Great Commission. God has also ordained that each person is a part of a family structure of some sort and this provides a perfect training ground to put this command into practice. Our goal is to reach as many people for Christ as possible and to help them grow to maturity in their relationship with Him. God has provided people in each of our lives that we can invest in, beginning with those closest to us. As we learn how to disciple those directly under our care, we will develop a skill set that can then be expanded to a hurting world outside of our homes.

Most of us are aware of the dismal statistics regarding the destruction of the family via divorce and the high percentage of young people rejecting Christ shortly after they leave the home. This tidal wave of failure must be addressed or we are in great danger of losing the bulk of an entire generation. Rather than just complain about the problem we want to move into solutions and become proactive.

Each person has a limited amount of time, and time is a resource that can only be spent once. In an Economics class in college, the instructor introduced to us the concept of "Opportunity Cost." This professor illustrated the concept with this sentence, "The cost of a McDonald's hamburger is not just the cost of the burger, but everything else we *could have* spent the money on." This sentence also rings true with our schedule and daily decisions. We can only spend an hour once and the cost is not only what we did with the time, but everything we *could have* done with it. We are stewards of time, as well as money, and we need to consider how we spend our non-replaceable resource called "time." What are we investing in? Discipleship should be high up on the list!

Many families are not placing as high of a priority on discipleship as they could or should. Perhaps the reason is that they feel they are doing enough by sending the children to a youth group or Sunday School class. Maybe there is a lack of understanding regarding the severity of the need and responsibility. In addition, some may lack the instruction or ideas in how to go about the process. The truth is that sending the children to a few hours of spiritual instruction a week, while helpful, is not enough to overcome the onslaught of evil and pressures from our world system. Additionally, our schedules must be reviewed to make sure that they are under the Lordship of Jesus Christ, and whatever is not needs to be removed.

What follows are multiple suggestions and ideas to help overcome the lack of knowledge or the fear of how to disciple those closest to us. Not every idea will work or even needs to be implemented, but almost everyone can and should do something to disciple those under their influence. Everyone is different so a "one-size-fits-all" approach does not work in the Kingdom of God. Below are some suggestions for each basic type of family unit. The goal is to begin the discipleship process if we have not, and if we have begun, to learn even more tools to assist in the journey of discipleship. We learn at home so we can make a greater difference as we step outside of it.

Singles

I want you to be free from anxieties. The unmarried man is anxious about the things of the Lord, how to please the Lord. But the married man is anxious about worldly things, how to please his wife, and his interests are divided. And the unmarried or betrothed woman is anxious about the things of the Lord, how to be holy in body and spirit. But the married woman is anxious about worldly things, how to please her husband. 1 Corinthians 7:32-34

Being a single adult provides the greatest freedom to serve Christ. The opportunities to travel, keep a flexible schedule, and develop a personal relationship with Jesus will open many doors for evangelism and discipleship. As a single adult, there is time to study the Word of God, listen to teachings, read, and serve without the time constraints of being married or raising children. If used properly, this period of life can provide the greatest opportunities for investing in others. So many single adults waste this stage of their life worrying about what they do not have (being married) instead of enjoy what they do have- an abundance of time to further the work of the Kingdom!

If you are a single adult, stop and take an inventory of the people in your life. Whom would the Lord have you invest more time in? Is there someone at work/school that is hurting or going through a difficult time? Perhaps other single friends need help or desire to grow spiritually. Would the Lord want you to consider leading a Bible or book study, prayer meeting, or beginning a service project to assist someone in need? Every situation can turn into a discipleship opportunity as you bring Christ into the time spent together with others. As you fill up your spirit with excellent teachings and your private devotional time, the Lord will bring others into your life so you can share with them what you are learning.

Consider investing in are those younger than you. If you are a single adult, there are most likely younger people that look up to you. Siblings or other young people in your church or social networks often idolize the single adult, and this provides an excellent opportunity to invest in the next generation. Leading a Bible study or simply spending time with younger people can pay tremendous dividends for the Kingdom of God. To realize how important this is, just remember how you felt when your older sibling or perhaps some other older young person reached out you. If that did not happen in your life, remember how you felt because it did not happen! You can make a difference in many people's lives if you invest your time properly.

If you will prepare yourself by study, prayer, and an investment of time, God will open doors for you to serve Him in marvelous ways. A young lady named Sarah was twenty-eight when she was married. Her older sister was married at age 20 and her younger brother at 21. Sarah wondered why she had not been asked to be married, struggling with what was wrong with her. Her parents shared Paul's exhortation recorded in 1 Corinthians 7, and she choose to invest her time in serving others while she waited for marriage.

During this time, Sarah traveled to China and worked in an orphanage, taught English in a high school, and was able to share her life with many foreign students. She went to cosmetology school in order to learn a useful skill, and she used this service to assist low-income families and continues to do so today. In her local church she became "Aunt Sarah" to a large number of young girls, ages 10-20 and invested her time in discipling them.

Sarah could often be seen before or after a church gathering surrounded by young girls hanging on her every word. She chose to invest herself in others rather than to think solely about herself or what she was missing. Eventually God brought in a wonderful young man that swept her off her feet and they were married. At Sarah's wedding, she had 40 young ladies singing as a choir, and there was not a dry eye in the house. Sarah used her singleness to help disciple many others and only eternity will reveal the full impact of her choice.

Sarah chose wisely, and so can you if you are single...invest in others and God will grant you the desires of your heart as they align with His (Psalm 37:4).

Husband

Paul stated in the verses above that once you are married you no longer live your life for yourself. There is now a spouse to consider, and this will radically change how you will live the rest of your days on earth. Marriage is a tremendous blessing, as well as one of hardest jobs in the world in which to excel. The Apostle Paul gives detailed instructions regarding marriage in Ephesians 5:22-33

> Wives, submit to your own husbands, as to the Lord. For the husband is the head of the wife even as Christ is the head of the church, his body, and is himself its Savior. Now as the church submits to Christ, so also wives should submit in everything to their husbands. Husbands, love your wives, as Christ loved the church and gave himself up for her, that he might sanctify her, having cleansed her by the washing of water with the word, so that he might present the church to himself in splendor, without spot or wrinkle or any such thing, that she might be holy and without blemish. In the same way husbands should love their wives as their own bodies. He who loves his wife loves himself. For no one ever hated his own flesh, but nourishes and cherishes it, just as Christ does the church, because we are members of his body. "Therefore a man shall leave his father and mother and hold fast to his wife, and the two shall become one flesh." This mystery is profound, and I am saying that it refers to Christ and the church. However, let each one of you love his wife as himself, and let the wife see that she respects her husband.

While not necessarily politically correct in our day, this is nonetheless the Word of God and must be considered prayerfully by every Christian, married, disciple. Beyond the specific instructions on how a marriage should function - husbands loving their wives by laying down their lives for them daily, and wives making sure they respect their imperfect husbands, some key insight is given into discipleship.

A husband should be helping to sanctify his wife by making sure she is "washed in the Word of God." The "in the same way" part of this Scripture passage gives insight for the husband on how to help disciple his wife. This may be intimidating to some men due to the wives being older in the Lord or perhaps not very receptive to the husband's leading, but the command is still there. Men are to learn to die for their wife, just as Christ did for the Church, and men are to make sure the Word of God is central in their homes.

Making the Lord the center of the home is a daily decision and a never-ending process. What currently dominates your home? The TV, Facebook, sports, or Christ? Husbands must be men of the Word in order to share the Scripture in their homes - Jesus said out of the abundance of our hearts our mouths speak (Matthew 12:34), so what is coming out of our mouths?

Making changes is not impossible, but there must be a willful decision if changes are to occur. If most meals are eaten together (which they should be if they are not), then this time allows the husband to lead in a prayer of thankfulness for the food and for the one that made it. In addition, this time could be used to bring up a discussion about what was read in private devotions or perhaps what each one believes God has taught during the day. Open-ended questions could be asked about a particular verse of Scripture or some potential problem the two of you are facing. Open ended means a question that cannot simply be answered with a "yes" or "no" answer. These type of questions are more of the "what" or "why" type questions. "Why do you think God allowed this to happen to Joe and Mary?" Or, "What do you think God is trying to tell us in reference to my job situation?"

You don't have to reinvent the wheel or be super creative. Try suggesting reading a book or listening to/watching a Christ-honoring program together and then discussing it. With the advent of the internet, there are unlimited resources available for you to consider if it is your desire to help your spouse grow in spiritual maturity. Biblically, husbands must take the lead in discipleship, and God will give you the ideas and grace to do so, if you will ask Him for it.

Another factor to consider is the tremendous power that is released by praying together with your wife.

Again I say to you, if two of you agree on earth about anything they ask, it will be done for them by my Father in heaven. Matthew 18:19

A husband that leads his wife in consistent prayer will increase her respect for him exponentially. Prayer allows for a deeper level of communication and will help to center the home in Christ. Even if the wife is not comfortable praying aloud, or, for that matter the husband either, praying together will help both grow spiritually. It may be awkward at first, but the comfort level will come and the home will change under the husband's leadership.

Discipleship may happen by chance, but it has a far greater potential to happen with a plan. If you seek the Lord about your responsibility and prayerfully ask Him for direction, He will give it. God brought your spouse into your life for a reason, and part of that reason was for you to care for her, nurture her, and help her grow in spiritual maturity.

Wife

A wife plays a crucial role in helping her husband grow and mature in the Lord (discipleship). She has the ability to build him up and help him become a strong man of God, or to destroy him. Solomon, who knew a little bit about wives, states it this way:

The wisest of women builds her house, but folly with her own hands tears it down. Proverbs 14:1

An excellent wife is the crown of her husband, but she who brings shame is like rottenness in his bones. Proverbs 12:4

Proverbs also states, "Life and death are in the power of the tongue," (Proverbs 18:21) and a wise wife will understand what she says to her husband will help or hinder his maturing. If the wife is older in the Lord, she should encourage her husband's growth by gently sharing insights she has learned from the Lord, and encouraging any efforts the husband displays in spiritual leadership.

The principle is to fan into flame any spark, not to pour water on it because it is small. The wise wife will praise and encourage her husband when he leads in prayer or Bible study and resist the temptation to comment about how immature or short it may have been. Husbands often have fragile egos and they need their wife's support, not criticism. Men do not like to be "slapped" or put down by their wife's comments and will often retreat into work, sports, or hobbies when they do not feel respected.

If the wife is younger in the Lord, she should encourage her husband by asking him questions and thus helping him to reinforce his leadership role. Something rises up in a man when he feels like he is fulfilling the role of being the leader, and this will spur additional desire for growth. A wise wife will help her husband become the man of God she desires rather than tear him down verbally.

In addition, the wife needs to be careful when discussing her husband with others. She will "bring shame" to him by exposing him to ridicule or by not protecting his reputation. Solomon stated this will result in "rottenness to the bones," and this is an apt picture. When a man finds out his wife is talking about him behind his back to others, he feels undermined, and the foundation is attacked. Bones hold the frame of our body up and by shaming her husband, she is causing damage to the structure. If she is complaining about his lack of leadership or perhaps some personal fault, once he knows he is the subject of the discussion with others, all motivation to change has been lost. Love covers a multitude of sins, and so will a wise wife. The husband that trusts in his wife will grow into a much better leader than the one that does not.

If both husband and wife will seek to be mature and to continue to grow in their own discipleship, they will ultimately end up assisting their spouse. The husband and the wife play a major role in the discipleship process to one another, and when a child arrives, the roles even expand.

Married With Children

When God blesses a couple with children (through either childbirth or adoption), the discipleship opportunities expand. In addition to what was stated above about the husbands' and wives roles, now there are additional lives involved. The same principles apply whether there are one child or a dozen regarding discipleship opportunities. The more children the greater the possible impact. Regardless of family size, each couple will have to adjust their lifestyle once a child or children arrive. The first requirement for godly parents is to accept the Biblical assignment regarding children:

> "Hear, O Israel: The Lord our God, the Lord is one. You shall love the Lord your God with all your heart and with all your soul and with all your might. And these words that I command you today shall be on your heart. You shall teach them diligently to your children, and shall talk of them when you sit in your house, and when you walk by the way, and when you lie down, and when

> you rise. You shall bind them as a sign on your hand, and they shall be as frontlets between your eyes. You shall write them on the doorposts of your house and on your gates.
> Deuteronomy 6:4-9

> Fathers, do not provoke your children to anger, but bring them up in the discipline and instruction of the Lord. Ephesians 6:4

God has delegated the training of the children to their parents. This is a phenomenal sentence if we consider the ramifications of it. God has entered into a partnership with parents and He expects them to fulfill their roles. The Lord has built into every Christian family the opportunity for hands-on discipleship practice. As a unified team, husbands and wives begin the process of training a child in the ways of the Lord. This will help prepare both the parents and the children to reach out to other potential disciples. In addition, if the parents do a good job discipling those in their own homes, the destructive trend of faith rejection can be turned.

We have already mentioned making sure both the husband and wife are growing spiritually in their own walk with the Lord, and this remains a focus after children arrive. Now the discipleship process needs to be enlarged to include the child(ren).

This can be accomplished in a variety of ways, a few of which have already been mentioned. First, the family schedule needs to be evaluated to assure the time is being spent in the most beneficial place. If it is not, then change must be made and the sooner the better. Second, mealtime offers a wonderful opportunity to bring Christ and the Scripture into the daily lives of each family member. Discussions can be planned or spontaneous, but make sure the Lord is a central figure in the conversations. Depending on ages of the children, topics can range from interpersonal relationship challenges to character development. The Scripture provides every answer to all questions either directly or in principle. Therefore, we must make sure that the Word of God is the center of our homes and always the ultimate resource for our answers.

Fathers can lead devotions around the meal table, in the living room or bedroom. These can be as deep as the level of understanding of the children. Bible stories can be read and discussed. Leading questions can be asked regarding moral choices, or characters' actions, and a lively discussion can be achieved. The goal is to provide an atmosphere where Christ is central and the Word of God is valued. In addition, insights can be shared from the daily devotions that each parent or child recently received. The Psalm or Proverb of the day also provides an abundance of material that can be read and discussed. The materials and ideas for a good discussion are only limited by the imagination.

Family worship times can help provide a growing discipleship environment in the home. If someone plays an instrument, chorus books or hymnals can then be used to lead in songs. If no one plays an instrument, then MP3's and CD's abound that contain wonderful worship songs to be enjoyed in the home. Worship is supposed to be a part of every day and not relegated to Sunday services only; leading our children in worship will help keep Christ as the center of our homes. The children need to see the reality of our walk with Jesus in order to want to follow in our footsteps.

Here are some other ideas to consider prayerfully

Mothers or fathers can read excellent books aloud to the family and then discuss them. These can cover any genre and could include classics like, *Pilgrims Progress* or *Pride and Prejudice*, fictional or actual history, end times thrillers, and a host of other type books. The book is not as important as the time spent together. Every discussion should focus on growing in Christ and obtaining a better understanding of how to walk with Him in our daily lives. The characters actions and thoughts can be evaluated and then their lives become object lessons to impart spiritual truth into our everyday lives.

Family prayer meetings can be called during times of crisis or when the Lord's specific direction is needed. Praying together and recording the request *and the* answer will help solidify the reality of Christ to the children. These times will often provide opportunities to explore issues like patience, waiting on God, what happens when God says, "no" to our prayers, etc. All of these are basic discipleship training issues. We teach our children to pray by praying. They will ultimately "catch" what is important to us by what we actually did, not necessarily what we said.

DVD's or movies can be watched and evaluated from a Biblical perspective. We are not to be naive or unaware of our adversary's schemes (Ephesians 6:11), and we should help our children process the entertainment they watch so they are growing in discernment as they mature. (Hebrews 5:14) Every book, movie, and song has an author who had a reason for writing what they did. These things may be germane in nature, but there is a spiritual side to everything and we must train our little disciples to grow in discernment.

Like any other discipleship relationship, the spending of time together is critical. A great deal of impartation and spiritual life takes place as you spend time doing the normal family activities. What is actually done is not as critical as the fact that a large amount of time is being spent together. Every parent looks for teachable moments, and the majority of these happen as large chunks of time are spent together. Very few people in nursing homes regret not spending more time at the office, yet they often regret that they cannot spend more time with their family. We can only spend time once, choose wisely.

Single Parents

In our current society, divorce is rampant and this has created a large group of single parents. Both men and women are now attempting to raise their children without a spouse to assist. Children often fall through the cracks of the broken home. As the single parent attempts to maintain a job and eventually seek another potential marriage partner, the children can be overlooked. Time is required and reprioritizing the schedule must be considered for the sake of the children. It is not their fault that the marriage fell apart, and they should not be deprived as a result. Single parents must attempt to fulfill the role of discipler even though they are now doing it alone. In fact, it is even more critical since the home is broken in two.

A single parent still has to invest in the lives of their children in the arena of discipleship. Reading books, praying together, Bible study, home worship, church membership, and such are needed for children of a single parent home. Children still spell love – T-I-M-E.

If the couple was Christian and divorced, the message has already been given to the children that the parents' Christianity was powerless to stop the divorce. This hurdle must be overcome in the discipleship process with the children. Even more time will need to be given to explain the marriage failure and why God did not intervene to prevent it. These issues provide a great opportunity to teach about forgiveness, patience, endurance, and many other desirable spiritual qualities.

Whether male or female, the single parent will need to supplement their discipleship process of their children with godly role models. The single parent will have to seek out others to include in their life to replace the spouse that is no longer there. Small groups, church involvement, gender-specific clubs or sporting programs can all assist in this process. The goal is to present to the child(ren) others that are excellent examples of Christianity and invite them into the process of discipleship with your children. Strong, godly friendships, extended family, and a committed church body, can all help to stem the damage caused by divorce.

Summary

The family unit is an excellent training ground for discipleship. It is often the most important, as well as the most overlooked regarding its potential. God created the family structure and He gave explicit details explaining how He expects it to function. If the Christian families would do a better job at discipling the children under their roofs, we would begin to see a reversal of the devastation of the family unit, the Church, and the nations. In addition, the large number of young people rejecting Christ as soon as they leave high school would begin to reverse. God spoke through the prophet Malachi the following:

> And this second thing you do. You cover the Lord's altar with tears, with weeping and groaning because he no longer regards the offering or accepts it with favor from your hand. But you say, "Why does he not?" Because the Lord was witness between you and the wife of your youth, to whom you have been faithless, though she is your companion and your wife by covenant. Did he not make them one, with a portion of the Spirit in their union? And what was the one God seeking? Godly offspring. So guard yourselves in your spirit, and let none of you be faithless to the wife of your youth. Malachi 2:13-15

The family unit is designed by God to propagate not only children but future disciples of Christ. Parents are given the honor and responsibility, from God, to invest wisely in the children under their care. While some of this process of discipling can be delegated to others to assist, the parents are still the ones that God will hold responsible for the discipleship. This is an awesome responsibility and the potential is amazing. God will empower and give grace to those that seek Him and walk in obedience to His commands. This includes the command to make disciples, beginning in the home.

The natural outworking of this process is forward looking. While it may seem that investing so much in the family is working against the spreading of the Gospel, the exact opposite is the truth. Since studies reflect a huge percentage of young people walking away from the faith, whatever investment is necessary to stop this bleeding is well worth the effort. If the 70-90% of young people leaving the faith upon entering college (as all studies reveal), could be reversed, or significantly reduced through helping the family unit function, the long term results would be overall growth of the Church at large.

In addition, as families begin to heal, refocus on Christ, and walk in discipleship, outreach will increase. A great deal of time and energy is currently being spent on recovery programs in the Church, but little on prevention. As marriages spiral into destruction, young people walk away in rebellion, and the overall condition of the family deteriorates even further, the Church and communities struggle to pick up the pieces.

If the tide of family destruction could be reduced significantly, these burdens would be relieved. Functional families can generate significant energy for the propagation of the Gospel, while dysfunctional ones drain it. Functional families require far less resources from the already overburdened churches, and actually can be released sooner into ministry. Healthy, growing, discipleship-oriented families will help reproduce more of the same kind, whereas, dysfunctional ones also reproduce more of their same kind. Which one offers the brightest hope for the future?

Since our goal is to walk in obedience to Jesus' final command - go and make disciples (Matthew 28:19), then the home is the first opportunity to learn how to walk in obedience to Jesus' command, and as I have strongly argued, it is the best place to invest for long term growth potential.

~~~~~~

Understand well the different tempers of your household and deal
with them as they are and as they can bear, not with all alike.
Richard Baxter (1615-1691)
~~~~~~

Children in the Pews?

But when Jesus saw it, he was indignant and said to them, "Let the children come to me; do not hinder them, for to such belongs the kingdom of God. Truly, I say to you, whoever does not receive the kingdom of God like a child shall not enter it." And he took them in his arms and blessed them, laying his hands on them. Mark 10:14-16

This passage of Scripture has always intrigued me. If you read the verses before this one you will see there were people (the disciples) rebuking the children telling them to be quiet, keep still, don't make noise, etc., and Jesus brushes past them and picks up the children and includes them into His teaching, not only that, he elevates the children to the position of role models.

Have you ever noticed children have an incredible knack for asking probing questions? They listen to a message and then ask questions that really challenge their parents. "What is faith, Daddy?" "How big is God, Mommy?" "The pastor said God could do anything, Daddy, why are you so upset about money?" We could probably learn a great deal from viewing God through the eyes of children.

In Jesus' day they did not have nurseries, children's church, or junior church, because families learned together. The children were part of everything, and they were taught to sit still and listen. The children learned from their parents' example.

Search the Scriptures diligently, but you will not find children isolated away from the parents during almost any congregational gathering. Why do so many parents and churches send them away today?

Sure, it takes discipline to train a baby or toddler to sit still. But it can be done. I believe it should be done! A child can sit and color for hours; surely they can sit for 30 to 40 minutes and listen to a message from the Word of God.

"But they won't understand the message," the parent states. True at first, but what a wonderful opportunity for the parent to explain what was said and what it means to the child. The result is the parent becomes wise in the child's eyes instead of a talking puppet or six-foot dog often used in children's ministry to explain the powerful truths of the Gospel.

If a message is "over their head," it gives the parents an opportunity to break it down to their level (teaching is the best way to learn!). By explaining it to a child, you will be sure you understand it as well! Some parents encourage their children to listen for key words and draw pictures of the main points. This keeps their attention, and, it really blesses me as their pastor when they come up after a service and share their pictures with me.

A father came to me one day after the service and said, "Your message wasn't very deep today." By God's grace I replied, "Well, what a wonderful opportunity for you to take the next six days and delve as deeply as you wish with your children. Begin where I ended and dig as deeply as you wish until next Sunday."

From that conversation, I began to encourage the parents to use my sermons as a launching point for their family devotionals or discussion times. Most of us that teach cannot possibly say everything about anything in one message. However, the parent can take what is shared and discuss it all week long with the family. What a blessing if every family member is hearing and discussing the same Scriptures all week!

Children need to see their parents worship, pray, take notes, and be involved with the service. We as parents teach much more by example than our words. "I just need a break from these kids," states the weary parent. Is the worship service really the proper (or best) time for the break? I know children can be tiring, but isn't the worship of God **THE** most important thing we should be teaching our children? Is this really the time to take a break and delegate it away to someone else?

I have worked with hundreds of teenagers over the last forty years. One common complaint is that they are bored in church. In the typical church, children are removed from the services beginning shortly after birth. They are fed crackers and juice in nurseries, then graduated to children's church, often entertained with loud noise, bright colorful puppets and video, and eventually moved into a youth type church with loud music, skits, and games, and finally, growing too old for the fun, they end up in big church - bored to tears. Every major study shows our young people are leaving the church in droves. Do we really have to wonder why? Some churches are attempting to change their services to accommodate the fleeing youth, but is that really the answer?

I believe a better, more Biblical answer, is to help train the parents to keep the children with them in the service. Train a child from birth to be part of something bigger than their own entertainment. Let the children see their parents taking notes, worshipping, and enjoying the church service. If we never expose them to the fast-paced, entertainment oriented ministry, they will not miss it when they are integrated into "big church," which, by the way, is where they will spend the rest of their lives if they walk with the Lord.

The children might even learn to enjoy listening, taking notes, worshipping and being part of both their own family and the family of God. As parents, I can think of no greater joy than introducing my children to the Lord and helping them grow in their faith, rather than isolating them into some remote corner of the building being trained by a stranger.

~~~~~~

So what is to be noted here is that heads of family must go to the trouble of being instructed in God's Word if they are to do their duty.

John Calvin (1509-1564)
~~~~~~

A Grandparent's Challenge

"Grandchildren are the crown of the aged, and the glory of children is their fathers." Proverbs 17:6

As I was sitting in the hospital room holding our fifth granddaughter, the revelation hit me that I was no longer a young man. I know it should have dawned on me sooner, but I was too busy to dwell on such things. Rapidly approaching sixty-four (and nine additional grandchildren later,) my thoughts yet again turn to those who will follow in my steps when I leave this earth for my reward. What am I leaving them? How will I be remembered?

When our first granddaughter arrived, there was an instant bonding between us, at least from my point of view. I held her in my arms and delight filled my heart as I gazed at that little girl. I marveled and rejoiced that I had lived to see this day.

At age 42, it was quite a jolt to be a grandfather, but it was a delightful shock! When Lydia arrived, my wife and I needed to evaluate our roles as grandparents. We were not her parents, yet there seemed to be something we were supposed to be doing beyond what the bumper stickers proclaimed about grandchildren (Spoiling them and sending them home, or spending their inheritance). There certainly was a strong generational connection, but we were not sure what our responsibilities were.

Those of us, who have given our lives for the raising of our children, can find it somewhat confusing as to our new roles as grandparents. As parents, we exercised almost complete control over our children until they were adults. Eating, sleeping, education, clothing and just about every other decision was made on behalf of the child, or at least in concert with them.

As our children grew, we were very involved right up until they left our home. Now, here is a newborn baby and the temptation is to resume our former roles. However, this must be resisted! These little ones are not ours, but belong to other parents who are just beginning the task we have completed. So what are we supposed to do as grandparents?

Here are a few lessons we have learned on this grandparent journey over the last twenty-one years. First, pray often for the new parents. They need wisdom and insight on how to adjust to the new family member and they will need an abundance of guidance as the child grows.

Second, be available to assist in babysitting, house cleaning, cooking, and any practical matter needed. Like so many, it would have been wonderful to have a night out now and again when our children were young. We simply did not have that option. Now we can provide that for our grown children, and they have all told us it is such a blessing!

Third, always remember to turn the heart of the child back to the parents. These precious gifts are not yours, but belong to their parents. Our job as grandparents is to reinforce what the parents want, not to contradict or undermine. Sometimes this can be challenging, because by the time we become grandparents we certainly have learned a few things from our experiences. We observe the mistakes of youth, and the temptation is to jump in and give an unsolicited opinion. A proverb I coined years ago goes like this:

> "Woe to the man who gives his opinion when it is not being asked, it will be reckoned unto him as a curse!"

If we develop a trusting relationship with our children as they age, our opinions will be asked for and valued when they are older and in need of our assistance. However, giving our opinion to our adult children before it is asked for will result in being labeled as a meddler and can damage your relationship for years.

One key point is that we must never undermine the parents to the grandchildren even if we disagree with the parents. If we observe harmful or dangerous behavior, then we must appeal to the parents discreetly, but never turn the hearts of the children away from their parents. We must reinforce what the parents are doing, not undercut it.

Remember what you wish your parents had done when you had your children still at home…then try to be that person! When a grandchild asks us for anything, if the parents are around, we always send them back to the parents, thus keeping the lines of authority clear. Grandparents that sneak behind the parents' backs are teaching rebellion and disrespect for authority, so we must be careful what we teach by our actions and attitudes!

As grandparents, we are modeling to another generation (whether we realize it or not) what it looks like to walk with God. Self-focused grandparents are missing a great opportunity to invest in the future. Our culture glorifies self-gratification and, unfortunately, many godly people have bought into this lifestyle without considering the outcome of this choice. The thought goes something like this: "I have lived my whole life raising my children, now I'm going to enjoy life and take care of me!" This lifestyle is evidenced by multitudes of grandparents moving to the coasts or deserts instead of staying by their families. From my perspective, this is a waste of experience and a loss to the next generation. Someone said years ago that very few people in nursing homes regret not spending more time at the office or on vacation, but almost all regret the time lost with their families. We never get to spend time twice so we must choose wisely the first time!

Even if you feel you have nothing to offer because your life has been full of mistakes, you have your love and experience to offer. One of the best ways to gain knowledge is by learning from other people's mistakes and then trying to avoid repeating them. How beneficial it would be for the older generation to pass on to the younger one the wisdom that was learned from all those mistakes! Do not waste them by keeping them all to yourself! Experiences should be passed on to those that follow us, both good and bad, for each possess a lesson or insight.

As grandparents, our goal should be to be godly examples that love and serve the next generation. We need to avoid violating the parents' authority and instead reinforce it to their children. We are not called to spoil grandchildren, but to help in the training process of them. We are blessed to enjoy this gift from God and take our responsibilities seriously and not simply live to gratify our flesh. Another generation is at stake and we must give ourselves selflessly to assist in capturing it for Christ!

I appeal to the grandparents (and future grandparents) to consider their involvement with the next generation. Is warmer weather really worth missing this opportunity? Playing golf and having abundant free time is great, but what about investing in your grandchildren or great-grandchildren? What about taking time to share your story with them? I love the ocean and taking walks enjoying breath-taking views, but I would rather not ever see them again than miss my grandchildren's lives! I can visit the ocean but moving away from my family is not an option. I would rather shovel ten feet of snow than miss the fellowship and joy of my children and grandchildren. Wouldn't you? Your family needs you more than the RV Park or your golf partners.

What could you do to help? How about offering to homeschool (tutor) the child or children one day a week for the frazzled mom? Perhaps babysitting occasionally to allow the parents a night out for pleasure or even some necessary shopping. Please consider writing out your personal testimony for the next generation, sharing some of your success stories or failures, focusing on what you learned from them. We all have so much to offer—may we not waste our knowledge! Please prayerfully consider where and how you live out the rest of your days. It is not too late to reengage in the battle, for the next generation is at stake!

~~~~~~

I know not how a minister can employ his time, studies, and pen better (next to the conviction and conversion of particular souls), than in pressing upon householders a care of the souls under their charge.

Oliver Heywood (1630-1702)
~~~~~~

Rebuilding Foundations

Discipleship is a hot topic of discussion, yet many statistics seem to reveal it is not being accomplished. With young people leaving the church in droves and divorce running rampant in the Church at large, there seems to be a gaping hole in the foundation.

The Church of Jesus Christ will not grow or multiply if we continue losing the next generation and if the foundations of marriage crumble. Psalm 11:3 presents an excellent question for church leaders to consider – *"If the foundations are destroyed, what can the righteous do?"*

The home is the seedbed for future leaders, provides training for functioning members, and the primary place for discipleship to take place. Yet, we all know the family unit as God intended is suffering. The question must be considered - what is the Church leadership going to do about it?

Ask just about any pastor or professional counselor what they spend the bulk of their time dealing with and family issues will be the top answer. Marriage issues, siblings not getting along, abuse, neglect, abandonment syndrome, and dysfunction are crippling the home. And discipleship. And ministry. And future leadership.

If we neglect the importance of helping those under our care to move their homes and marriages from dysfunction to function, we are missing a golden opportunity for leadership and discipleship. A wide variety of ministry will take place from and within a functioning home. How much takes place in one trapped in dysfunction?

The Scriptures provide a key to reviving the home and Church. Consider these few for starters:

- And these words that I command you today shall be on your heart. You shall teach them diligently to your children, and shall talk of them when you sit in your house, and when you walk by the way, and when you lie down, and when you rise. You shall bind them as a sign on your hand, and they shall be as frontlets between your eyes. You shall write them on the doorposts of your house and on your gates.
  Deuteronomy 6:6-9

- He must manage his own household well, with all dignity keeping his children submissive, for if someone does not know how to manage his own household, how will he care for God's church? 1 Timothy 3:4, 5
- An elder must be blameless, the husband of but one wife, a man whose children believe and are not open to the charge of being wild and disobedient. Titus 1:6 NIV

There are many more of course, but these passages should lead us to consider what we are doing in helping to restore function to the home.

Moses, in essence, said, if you are awake you should be teaching. Though we may delegate some of the teaching to others, God will hold the parents responsible for what is being taught to their children. Many parents miss an excellent opportunity for discipleship right around their table. As we age we know children grow up quickly and our window for direct influence closes. What would happen if the majority of families within the Church took this opportunity seriously?

We seem to forget or even overlook the fact the Paul stated that one requirement for an elder/pastor was to have his family in order, well-managed, children under control, etc. In fact, Paul explained to his young disciples Timothy and Titus that how a man led in his home was a very good reflection of how he would lead the Church. Would we ever consider disqualifying someone due to how they lead their family? Should we? Shouldn't a leader be at least partially evaluated by their followers' imitation of them? Isn't this even more true when those followers are family members?

What would the Church look like if there were even a ten percent decrease in family dysfunction? What if that percentage increased to twenty, thirty or more? Would the Church be better off? Isn't it worth some time and energy to purposefully instruct the Church members to practice discipleship in the home?

If we don't begin to reverse the trends, the foundations will crumble, then where will we be?

Choose Your Friends Wisely

Proverbs 13:20 - *"He who walks with the wise grows wise, but a companion of fools suffers harm."* If you are concerned about whom your children run with, you have probably been accused of being overprotective. Well, we are protective, but are we overprotective? It seems to me that one of our jobs is to ensure that our children (or our spouses or ourselves!) do not have fools for companions.

There is a real enemy who hates you and your family. His mission is to destroy you anyway he can, through any means possible. One of the oldest tricks in the book is to add a fool to your family. A fool is not a simpleton, or someone with a low IQ, but someone who says there is no God, or does not honor God with his or her lifestyle. The Devil will try to lead you astray through the company you keep, or those you allow the members of your household to be around.

Paul said in I Cor. 15:33 *"Do not be misled: Bad company corrupts good morals or character."* There is a price to pay for allowing a "fool" into your family's life. We must be careful whom we allow our children to associate with. Our children are so impressionable. We need to know who is making the impression, and what that impression is!

Should you allow your child to spend the night with someone? How long should I allow my child out of my sight without checking on him? Should I be constantly watching our bad attitudes? If I see an attitude problem, should I find out where it came from? All of these questions, and hundreds more, should go through your mind as a parent. God will hold us responsible for the influences we allow into our children's lives from TV, books, the web, and friends.

The friends we should encourage our children to be with are those who will challenge them to walk with the Lord. Friends who will pull them up to a higher calling, not drag them down into mediocrity. Our children need good role models, godly role models who reinforce what we are teaching them at home, not "friends" who tell them "your parents are so weird," or "your parents are so strict," etc.

Choosing whom you interact with on a regular basis can be one of the most important decisions you ever make! A wise man will hang around with wise men, and will become still wiser. A fool will hang around with fools, and sink even farther.

I've often said, "the big difference between a child who avoids trouble and the child who ends up in trouble, is one word: "supervision."

When we make a commitment to be actively involved in the lives of our children, we are on our way to success. We must know whom our children are with. What type of influence are they? Do they encourage my children to respect me, or reject my authority? Do they encourage them to walk with the Lord, or to try the "forbidden fruit"? When I do allow my children to spend the night, how do they come home? Does it require hours of "deprogramming"" Did they watch movies and do activities I would not have approved of if they had taken place in my home? Do they come home with a good report?

All of this may seem like too much bother, but the stakes are incredibly high! Our children are at risk. We are given the task to see to it they choose wisely, and make good friends. Bad company will corrupt good morals. It rarely works the other way around!

Proverbs 27:23 - *"Know well the condition of your flocks."* I believe this applies to our families. We need to be involved enough to see the dangers and hide our families and ourselves. We need to see the influences in our children's lives and help them make the correct decision. If we pay the price now and help them make good decisions when they are young, we will save ourselves (and them!) much grief when they are older.

Proverbs 29:15 - *"A child left to himself will bring shame to his mother."* We do not have to do much to fail as parents. Just leave our children alone. We must help them choose correctly until they are able to choose on their own. Let's see to it that our children do not walk with fools, but with the wise. Then they will be wise when they grow up, and can train their children to be wise after them.

~~~~~~

Young persons are often each other's tempters and destroyers. The lewd and profane tempt others to lewdness and profaneness…And, as if it were not enough to ruin their own souls, many thus contract the guilt of assisting to destroy those of their companions and friends.

J. G. Pike (1784-1854)
~~~~~~

Finding a Spouse

*"He who finds a wife finds a good thing
and obtains favor from the LORD" – Proverbs 18:22*

What do you do with crushes, rejection, flirtation, and hormones? If you are even barely involved as a parent, you will notice your children will be attracted to someone of the opposite sex beginning at a young age. This is a God-given desire and the primary reason most folks end up getting married. The attraction issue is not the problem for most parents, but what do you do with it, and when. In my opinion, allowing a child to become involved with someone of the opposite sex before they are ready to get married is a tragedy waiting to happen.

Parents need to begin the discussion about what your goals are with your children in this critical area while they are young. We had two goals-- moral purity, and parental involvement. We began very early to tell our children it is perfectly normal to feel attracted to someone, or to like them, but it is not okay to go anywhere with it. If God wants you to marry that person then the desire will remain and that person will return it in the proper time. The key here is parental involvement --knowing what your child is going through and understanding what struggles they are having, will assist you in helping them to process it all.

We often discussed the importance of not allowing yourself to be in a place of temptation, for I believe it is easier to avoid temptation than to overcome it. We had many family friends when our children were growing up that had children of the opposite sex. Many enjoyable evenings were spent with coed activities. The main way we dealt with the boy-girl issue when our children were still at home was to usually do whatever we were doing together as a family, thus allowing close parental supervision. "Good children" still want to explore sexually and they come equipped with hormones. Leaving boys and girls alone for extended periods of time is unwise no matter how innocent you think they are.

One key to many of these difficult issues is communication. No amount of religious activity will replace the necessity of talking with your children for hours on end. In order for there to be effective relationships, vast amounts of time must be spent in discussion. There are no shortcuts to this process. If you want good fruit, you cannot get it any other way than to invest the time required.

As our children age, it becomes necessary to determine which philosophical view we will use in finding a marriage partner. The Scripture is not clear as to the preferred method of finding a spouse. Using historical narrative to base your understanding or preference on is potentially dangerous. The Benjaminites in Judges 21 captured dancing girls at a religious festival and ran off with them. Rich men would buy slaves, and many times parents would select the mate. Wives could be gained as "plunder" from war, or bartered over between fathers or older brothers. Any of the above methods could be considered "Biblical," however, I would not recommend them.

The Two Models

The two primary choices we face in our day are dating, versus some sort of courtship, and both require a bit of explanation.

Dating typical involves a young man and woman spending time together paired up with no long term commitment or view towards marriage. A different guy or girl could pair up each night or weekend and go to a movie or out to eat for the sheer fun of it. Perhaps it will lead to a deeper commitment or maybe not. The point is to enjoy the time together and see what happens. After dating for a time, marriage may become the goal of the relationship, but it is not the initial one.

Courtship typically involves a couple not pairing up unless marriage is the ultimate goal. There are as many understandings of courtship as there are dating. Some parents are very involved and others are not. Some lean to prearranged marriages and some to a more flexible system. The main difference between courtship and dating is the end goal of the pairing of the couple.

For our family, we chose a courtship understanding in light of our two goals stated previously – moral purity and parental involvement. All three of our children married and we actually had five courtship experiences. All five worked to varying degrees, and we learned a great deal through each of them.

Our first born was subjected to a very strict, narrow understanding of courtship. Her husband practically had to sign a document stating he intended to marry our daughter before I would let him even meet her! It seems like many parents experiment on our firstborns, and I am sure there is a special reward in heaven for all of them!

The young man's father called me one day and asked if I would be willing to have lunch with him and his son. The son was away at college and could not find a girl that wanted to stay at home and be a mom. All the girls at college were very forward and not what he was interested in at all. His dad told him he knew of such a girl that might just work. We had a great lunch lasting about three hours and began the process of interviewing. I really did not know what I was doing, but I knew it was my job to "screen" out undesirable young men.

For months, Brian and I wrote back and forth and I was able to get to know him at a deep level. I had always told my daughters to look for two qualities in a young man – teachableness and kindness. Good looks and muscles will fade, but these two traits will only get better as the years pass. Brian had both of them in abundance! Of course, he was not too bad looking either! Over the next year or so, they fell in love and married. We attempted to provide encouragement, supervision, and assistance as they entered into the engagement process.

In addition to looking for certain character qualities, like teachableness and kindness, I encouraged my children to observe their prospective mate interaction with their family. How does the young man or woman interact with their parents and siblings? Are they respectful or rebellious? Are they inclusive and loving with their siblings, or nasty and hateful? The parents and children are this person's family. After you say, "I do," you become their family as well. The way they treat their family now is a good indication of how they will treat you after you become family. Choose wisely.

My son actually had two courtship experiences. One was with a wonderful girl that we had known for many years. They entered into the courtship to determine if marriage was what God had for them. After a period of time, it became clear this was not God's will for either of them. While painful, the courtship was ended. Both ended up marrying others that were more suitable. Even though the courtship did not end in marriage, the goal of the relationship was not simply pleasure oriented, but an honest evaluation of marriage suitability.

My middle daughter also had two courtship experiences. One ended similarly to our son's, and the other resulted in an excellent marriage with a delightful young man. Sarah, was 28 when she married and this provided her many opportunities to travel and serve before becoming a wife. As Sarah watched her older sister and younger brother marry, the natural questions were asked, "What is wrong with me? Why am I not married?" Our counsel to her was to follow Paul's instructions to singles in 1 Corinthians 7 – be wholly devoted to the Lord and be concerned with investing in others while you wait.

Our daughter did this wonderfully, and we were extremely proud of her. It was not always easy, but she decided to spend her time serving. She travelled to China to teach and assist a missionary. She became a cosmetologist so she could provide a necessary service to families that didn't have a lot of money. And, she invested in the young girls in our church. Sarah became "Auntie Sarah" to about 40 young girls. These same girls all were invited to sing as a choir in her wedding when the day finally arrived. It was quite a sight, and brought tears to just about everyone's eyes. Only God knows the eternal impact made by one older daughter being willing to invest in the lives of young girls!

Courtship is not a magic solution and is no guarantee your children will not have struggles morally or will have a successful marriage. Every child grows up and becomes an adult that is fully capable of making foolish, sinful decisions. Only Jesus is perfect and only He lived a sinless life. Adult children can and do fall. As parents of adult children, we must be there to help them recover and pick up the pieces as God supplies the grace.

We chose courtship over dating because my wife and I were products of the dating system. From our perspective, dating prepares a person for divorce, not marriage. The selfish, pleasure-seeking aspect of dating does not properly prepare someone for the death-to-self traits necessary for marriage. Spending time with someone and becoming emotionally and/or physically entangled, and then simply walking away for someone else, does not produce stability or the commitment necessary to survive in our world. Divorce is rampant in the Church, and perhaps one reason is that we are following the world's method of casual partner-swapping. Marriage is hard work and takes deep commitment in order to succeed.

Whatever method you choose to follow, parental involvement should be the goal, and of course, moral purity. Many marriage issues that require years of counseling to overcome begin during the pre-marriage relationship. Sexual exploration and experimentation, while pleasurable for the couple, often leads to long term problems. Sexual sin is the one sin that we are told to run from and the reason is obvious: it is extremely difficult to resist in the heat of the moment. One sure way to avoid sexual failure is to take along a younger sibling or never allow yourself to be in a place where you cannot be interrupted. Pulling off on a side road and getting into the back seat of a car will not help you avoid sexual failure, unless you're younger brother is back there!

Sometimes young people fall in love and press ahead in marrying their choice regardless of parental cautions or objections. In regards to selection of a life partner for marriage, I have yet to meet anyone that did not sooner or later regret their decision to rebel against their parents, and if they could do it over again, they would not have done so. I have worked with hundreds of people that do regret their foolish choice, and they wished they could go back and change it. Even if their marriage is successful, they live with a nagging regret that they did not have their parents' blessing on the union. Often though, their marriages are riddled with guilt and difficulties stemming from the pride and arrogance of not properly dealing with parent's objections.

Many times parents have God-given insight into the difficulties that the marriage will encounter, and any couple that is trying to follow the Lord will want their parents' blessing on that marriage. Pushing ahead without their consent will dishonor them and make for a very rocky marriage. The demanding of my own way, over the objections of the parents, also is a confession of unbelief. In essence, this action is stating that God is simply unable to change the parental authority to agree with your direction, so then you must take action. It is far better to pray and allow God to change your parent's (or your!) heart, than to press on with the marriage.

Choosing a life partner is a momentous decision. I have often stated, "It is far better to be happily married for forty years, than to be miserably married for fifty." If it takes ten years to find the right mate, you will not regret the time spent in waiting.

While waiting, I would highly recommend to the young person to work on becoming a desirable marriage partner rather than worrying about where their beloved will come from, and when their future spouse will arrive.

God is Sovereign even involving future marriages! Don't worry or be fearful, but prepare yourself by becoming a mature believer full of good works and excellent character qualities. God can handle it!

What about Education?

Do we homeschool our children or let the public schools do it for us? Perhaps we should look for a small, private school to bridge the gap between these two main choices. This is not a small question, and the way we answer it depends on what our goal and vision is for our family.

Today, we have several choices as parents - We can send our children to the public schools (I prefer to call them government ones!), or we can choose to go an alternative route in choosing between home education and private schools. Let's look at the last two options for a bit.

The Christian/Private school movement arose to combat the government schools' indoctrination and poor test results, and has been around for many years now. Most Christian/Private schools are excellent academically and are populated with dedicated teachers and administrators. They boast of smaller class sizes and teacher pupil ratios and are still growing rapidly in pupils served.

In the late 1970's and early 1980's Home Education was birthed by parents wishing to maintain significant control over, not only the academics, but also the influences that were affecting their children.

These dedicated parents choose to keep their children home and attempted to take on the task of teaching their own children, usually around the dining room table or in the living room. The risks were considerable in these days, resources were scarce, and those that freely educate their children today owe a good deal to these brave pioneers. From the humble beginnings of hiding in the home for fear of the truant officer knocking on the door, to national conferences and endorsements galore, the movement has come into its own.

In making this all important education choice, parents must research their options, know their children intimately, and understand the *consequences* for their decision. Each of the three main options has strengths and weaknesses to be considered.

Government schools have the advantage of significant resources including books, facilities, staff, transportation, and diverse athletic and extracurricular actives for free (I know we are taxed for it, but we really don't have any say over that, now do we?) or relatively inexpensive cost. The classrooms are typically well equipped, and the teaching staff is trained via rigorous educational programs.

On the downside, however, these schools attempt to pass on worldviews that are highly offensive to many parents, and given the nature of group dynamics, the classroom will typically gravitate to the slightly below average student. Peer dependence is often the norm, and many children are scarred for life from experiences during their years in school. In addition, the romantic interaction between boys and girls, and now gender-neutral or blurred is typical and encouraged at all levels and often leads to many broken hearts and worse.

The Christian/Private school option typically provides excellent academic training often producing significantly higher scores than the government schools on standardized testing. The staff and administration usually are dedicated professionals who love the students and consider their work to be a ministry.

Parents who send their children to these schools do not have to worry about their children being exposed to the same philosophic-oriented materials presented in the government schools.

The drawbacks include expensive tuition, limited sports and extracurricular activities, and the same group dynamics of classroom instruction and peer-dominated relationships in the age-segregated government schools. The romantic notion between the sexes is also dominant in this education choice.

Parents who choose to home educate their children desire to maintain a greater control over both the academic and philosophic influences their children are exposed to in the other two models.

Recent studies show that the home-educated children are beating the test scores of even the private schools in the nationalized testing, at costs significantly less than either of the other two options. One reason for this is that there simply is nowhere to hide when sitting at the table with the parent. The student either knows the answer or does not. In the organized school, the ability to duck behind someone's head to avoid eye contact is routinely used to get by in the classroom.

One-on-one tutoring in the home school provides immediate feedback, and the group dynamics of sinking to the middle of the class academically are avoided. Children can go as fast as they want or spend as much time as they need in order to grasp the subject at hand. Freedom of schedule and ease of communication enhance the education process.

In addition, societal issues can be controlled by the parents. Children can be exposed to (or not) whatever the parents desire, whenever they deem the children ready to see or hear it, including the natural attraction between the sexes.

Like the other two options there are some drawbacks with home education. Significant time is invested in teaching, lesson planning, grading and evaluation of the work, outings, and curriculum evaluation. Sometimes a lack of expertise in certain subjects like math or science can also hinder the students' learning potential. Most home schools are not equipped for extracurricular activities like sports and band; however, some support groups are attempting to address this issue by pooling their resources and partnering with small schools.

We home educated our children all the way through high school, and I highly recommend it. The choice to do so was made primarily because we desired to be their main influence in all matters both academic and social. The cost of time and effort is significant, and home education should not be entered into lightly. Choosing this option will take time, energy, and many life style changes.

With the advent of the internet and the explosion of resources now available for those who desire to home educate, there really is no reason not to attempt it if at all possible. Parents that want to spend more time with their children, learn a great deal more than they did in their schooling, and enjoy the experience of watching their children grow, should pursue home education.

Our family vision was the driving force in the education decision, and so should yours be. The choice to send your children away for large parts of the day should not be made without considering the consequences of that action. I believe we are free to delegate away some of the duties we are given as parents, but we will never be absolved of the responsibility of that action. If you choose to delegate the education of your children to either a government or Christian/Private school, you are still held responsible for what they are taught and will have to invest many hours to help your children process what you really didn't want them to learn in the first place.

I also understand that sometimes parents have little to no choice over the education of their children. Divorce and premature death of a spouse can severely limit education choices. As always, faith and dependence on our loving Heavenly Father will provide direction and rest even in the face of less than desirable choices.

A Public Service Announcement For Parents

PAD - a new threat is sweeping the church of America...in reality it is not all that new for it has been around as long as there have been parents and children...this syndrome can infect any family at any time...this hideous monster strikes and often leaves irreparable damage in its wake.

Sometimes the results of this vile outbreak include broken hearts, damaged spirits, disastrous choices, division, strife, and sin patterns that influence the victims for life. **PAD** often sneaks up on unsuspecting victims and wreaks its havoc before it is even diagnosed. This easily cured disorder is often not even considered when a family is facing major relational issues, and is ignored at the family's own regret.

Countless teenage pregnancies and immoral behavior of all sorts including porn addiction find their roots in this terrible threat! Unchecked lying, stealing, deceit, poor work ethics, poor choices of marriage partners, and even failing school grades have their roots in **PAD**. While I am not normally an alarmist, I believe this outbreak has, and can, ruin any family! We must take action today. We must be alert! We must resist the rampant spread of **PAD**.

PAD cannot be defeated with vitamins, oils, exercise, or modern medicine. There is only one known cure, and while relatively easy to administer, it is strongly resisted by many. Often attempts are made to counter **PAD** with money, possessions, and busyness, but all prove futile in the end. There is however, one cure that is effective, and it is completely backed by the Creator.

What is **PAD** you may wonder? **Parental Attention Disorder**. When we as parents are too busy to invest in the lives of our children we release this horrid, terrible, disastrous, devastating, debilitating, dreadful, ruinous, catastrophic, generational-influencing, (well you get the idea) life-long impacting disorder. Our family, our churches, and our nation suffer because of the choices we make as parents!

The cure is simple, but costly. We must rearrange the priorities of our life. The gift God has given us in our children and grandchildren must be guarded, and our time and oversight must increase in their lives.

- Do we know what they are thinking?

- Do we know whom they are playing with, and how they are playing? What they are saying?
- Do we know where they are?
- Do we know what they are listening to and watching on the computer and TV?

How can we train them if we are not with them? How can we correct behavior that needs direction if we do not know what they are doing and how they are doing it? How can we pray for them with insight if we are not spending time with them and talking with them? We cannot and must not delegate this God-given task to others! While others can and do assist, the responsibility has been given to you as the parents from The Creator Himself!

PAD is lurking near your home...are you prepared to deal with it? The cure rests in parental action taken...and the sooner the better! The results of this disorder can be repaired, but action must take place **ASAP!** Act now to limit the outbreak and spread of this sickness! While there are no 100% guarantees that our children will always make the correct decisions, they stand a much better chance of success if we fight **PAD** daily! An involved and informed parent will help limit the impact of this dreaded disorder in our society.

This has been a public service message from one who has been fighting the results of this terrible disorder for the better part of his life...parents, be aware, and take action today to protect your family from **PAD**!

See: - Psalm 127:3-5, Proverbs 17:6, 22:6, 29:15, Ephesians 5:16, 6:4. Philippians 4:8, Hebrews 12:5-11 for directions to help combat **PAD**.

~~~~~~

In all your conduct, manifest the most undeviating consistency. Children, even at a very early age, are eagle-eyed to observe the inconsistencies of a parent.
James Cameron (1809-1873)

Train with this thought continually before your eyes- that the soul of your child is the first thing to be considered.
J. C. Ryle (1816-1900)
~~~~~~

About the Author

Dr. Jeff Klick has been in fulltime church ministry since 1981. He serves as the senior pastor at Hope Family Fellowship in Kansas City, Kansas, a church he planted in 1993. Dr. Klick married his high school sweetheart, Leslie, in May of 1975. They have three adult children and fourteen grandchildren. Dr. Klick loves to learn and has earned a professional designation, Certified Financial Planner, earned a Master's degree in Pastoral Ministry from Liberty Theological Seminary, a Doctorate in Biblical Studies from Master's International School of Divinity, and a Ph.D. in Pastoral Ministry from Trinity Theological Seminary. In addition to serving as senior pastor at Hope Family Fellowship, Dr. Klick is a consultant with The Institute for Church Management and also serves on the Board of Directors for The Council for Gospel Legacy Churches. www.jeffklick.com

Jeff's Other Books (available at Amazon.com in print/Kindle)

Courage to Flee, Second Edition - How to achieve and keep moral freedom.

Gospel Legacy: A Church and Family Model - God's plan for the family explained from a Biblical perspective.

The Master's Handiwork - God is not finished with any of us yet and He never fails, so don't give up or in.

Reaching the Next Generation for Christ: The Biblical Role of the Family and Church - Detailed research on faith impartation to the next generation.

The Discipling Church: Our Great Commission - An in-depth study and training guide on the Great Commission.

A Glimpse Behind the Calling: The Life of a Pastor - Written to help both pastors and those who love them.

For Our Consideration: Food for the Christian Mind – Sixty devotionals and eight in-depth Bible studies to assist parents, small groups or anyone wanting to dig deep into the Word of God.

Love in the Face of Life – A practical guide to learn how to walk in 1 Corinthians 13 love.

Pastoral Helmsmanship, Confessions of a Church Felon, Navigating Conflict Three books co-authored to specifically assist church leaders.

Made in the USA
Middletown, DE
21 July 2019